dare to be different

HOW TO CREATE BUSINESS ADVANTAGE THROUGH INNOVATION AND UNIQUE SELLING PROPOSITIONS

Alessandro Forte

CONTENTS

ABOUT THE AUTHOR

Sandro (as he prefers to be known) was born in 1968; the eldest of four children to Leo, a successful restaurateur, and Carol. During a fairly ordinary education he had, at various times, decided to be a doctor, teacher, actor and policeman. By the time he left a three year University and drama school degree course he was only certain about one thing – he had to find a way to pay off his student overdraft.

His determination to do so took him back to his home town of Weston-super-Mare where a chance meeting with a family friend, who had just started his own financial consultancy practice, took him into the life insurance business.

After getting no-where fast Sandro decided to move from an administrative role to one that involved selling; something completely new to him. Starting out with no more than twelve contacts he took nearly three years to make anything like a decent living. By then, however, he had spent a considerable amount of time studying the books and tapes from most of the good business practitioners and suddenly he was qualifying for Million Dollar Round Table (MDRT) Top Of The Table; MDRT being the premier organisation for life insurance people and the organisation's Top Of The Table representing the top 0.25% of insurance sales people in the World.

His unprecedented success as a salesman led to invitations to speak at Life Insurance Association meetings around the United Kingdom and then, more significantly, at their 2000 Annual Convention in London. Many other invitations followed including the prestigious Main Platform at MDRT and from other sales and business organisations from as far afield as Malaysia, South Africa, Singapore, Canada, Israel, France, Thailand, Holland, Taiwan and Australia.

Now regarded as one of the great 'new age' business practitioners and speakers Sandro is in considerable demand to share his innovative, yet simple and transferable, ideas with others.

His hobbies include golf, football, travelling and the theatre. What spare time he has is spent with his wife Ruth and twin children Thomas and Ellie.

FOREWARD

In 1976, when I was just seven years old, my dad – who was a wonderful, caring man – was diagnosed with lung cancer. It was terminal. I was only a small boy at the time so I didn't understand the horrors my father would face as he fought the disease.

Sadly, he passed away two years later. He left my mum and four children – I was the eldest. During his life, he had built up an excellent restaurant business. We lived in a big house and wanted for nothing. But under the terms of a family agreement the business passed to his sister; my mum was left with the house but, significantly, no other financial provision. It was inevitable she couldn't afford to run the house and, within two years, it was sold to pay mounting debts and the five of us were moved into welfare housing – a two bedroomed property.

As sometimes happens, when one door closes in life another seems to open and, shortly after, my mum met Dave; an equally lovely man whom I came to think of as my own father. But during the time I was growing up I had always promised myself I would never let my family go through the same experience again so, when I came into the life insurance business in 1989 I had the opportunity to ensure there was money available for the family if the worst happened; if lightning were to strike twice.

How many times have we put off approaching someone for fear of rejection – especially rejection from someone we love? For two years I put it off. My own parents needed life insurance – the number of children had now grown to seven – but I found myself guilty of procrastinating; pre-determining what they would say if I approached them.

Could lightning strike twice? Of course I hoped not, but could I really stand back and watch my mother go through the same thing again if it did?

I'd promised myself, I would see this one through, to at least talk to them about the cover I knew they needed. I was then 24 years old but the youngest of the seven children was only 3. The first thing Dave said was they could never afford the premiums and there were plenty of other things they'd rather be doing with what little money they had. For once, I didn't walk away from a 'knock-back' but simply suggested we submit a proposal to see what terms were offered. A little reluctantly Dave agreed, although he said he wasn't promising anything. In truth, I think he liked the idea of a free medical – but during tests was found to have diabetes. He wasn't far off being uninsurable but I managed to get terms – a 300% premium increase – and then attempted to explain to them there was now even more reason to invest in the insurance because insurance companies don't tend to increase premiums unless there is an increased need for cover. But at three times the premium I knew I might be fighting a lost cause. Of course, I worried about them affording the premiums but, after much discussion, they agreed: they agreed because they knew what the financial implications would be if lightning **did** strike twice. I'd kept my promise but, more than anything else, I'd done the right thing. I knew my mum could now sleep just a bit easier at night………

Then our world fell apart.

Only two months after taking out the policy Dave fell ill. Dave was diagnosed with stomach cancer. I couldn't believe it was happening to us again. This time, though, the cancer was very progressive. It had apparently been there for some time masked, ironically, by the symptoms of the diabetes. There was to be no two year battle for him. Within a week he was in hospital and just four days later he was dying. As I sat alone by his bedside one day he was drifting in and out of consciousness. Finally, with failing strength, he whispered to me "Son, thank you for what you did for your family. I'm so proud of you". Those were the last words he ever spoke.

In many ways I'm lucky. I realise that's not the sort of thing one would expect me to say but it's true. If I could turn back time I would, of course. But I can't. So I'm left to reflect on whether I would actually have what I have now if things had been different. Would I still be in the financial services business? Unlikely. Would I be married to a wonderful lady and have two beautiful children? Probably not. Fate is a strange thing.

Sometimes, a profoundly tragic experience like the one I suffered – along with the rest of my family – can have a positive impact on one's life. For me, that manifested itself as a focus and determination to succeed; starting with telling everyone I could about what had happened to us and, in the process, encouraging them to take positive action in dealing with their own financial affairs.

This book isn't just about my 'story'. After all, many people have endured similar experiences. Rather, it is about the practical application of a number of ideas which transformed a very ordinary business (I had spent quite a few years in the business 'wilderness') into something creative and highly successful. The insurance policy I sold to my parents has meant my mum, now married for a third time, has the financial security I have always tried to advocate.

I'm very proud to have been asked to share these ideas; both to audiences around the world and now in the form of a book.

I have been thinking about this book for some time but it was only when I got asked on the several hundredth occasion whether I was going to commit my sales and business ideas to text that I set the goal and started writing.

Now that I have done what I set out to do I have the opportunity to publicly thank some of the (many) people who have made this book possible.

Firstly I want to thank my parents – all of them; including my aunt – for the sacrifices they made and the unwavering support they gave me during some rather 'colourful' formative years. To the Metcalfes, Deakins, Isaacs and Hall-Scotts – good friends who always keep me smiling. To the many people who helped me put this book together; not least my long suffering Personal Assistant Tina Robins who has been with me almost from the beginning and who never seemed to get fed up with all the re-writes and corrections. To my wife Ruth for her love, support and encouragement – even during the difficult times.

I also want to thank the many people whose ideas I have used to good effect and to the vast number of friends I have made around the world; not least Tony Gordon - one of the true greats of the Life Insurance business and who was so kind to me in helping me develop my speaking engagements.

Lastly, I want to thank you for investing in this book. I hope that, as a result of reading it, you feel inspired enough to take the action that will undoubtedly make a difference to your life and the lives of others.

DEDICATION

This book is dedicated to my wife, Ruth; without whom I would not have had the courage and determination to achieve anything……

CHAPTER ONE – IT'S NOT WHAT YOU KNOW, IT'S WHAT YOU DO

We live in an ever-changing environment and nothing changes more so than the business world.

Some of the technological advances, particularly in recent years, have been staggering. In a split second, we can now communicate with pretty much anyone, anywhere, on the planet. We can buy most goods and services via a computer. We are even close to putting the first person on Mars. Thanks to the development of medical practice we are now living longer than ever; we are better educated than at any other time and we are now building bigger houses and bigger businesses.

Has this all happened overnight? Of course not. The process of change has been with us since time began; which leads us to ask - almost inevitably - why do we find change such a tough nut to crack? We weren't born successful, any more than we were born as failures. We weren't born positive or negative, self disciplined or enthusiastic. Most of all, we weren't born with what we have today. Where we are right now is a direct result of change.

Often, when I am addressing the audience at a business meeting or convention, I have them draw a vertical line down the centre of a piece of paper. Then I ask them to sign their name as many times as they can in the left hand column in thirty seconds – as if they were taking part in a world signature-signing competition and they were going for the gold medal. In fact, if you have some paper and a pen handy try it now. You have thirty seconds and when you are finished, total your score.

The challenge now is to beat your best in the right hand column. You have the same amount of time – a strict thirty seconds – but this time you know what you have to beat. Do you think you can eclipse your best? Are you totally focused? Are you ready? Before you begin, however, transfer the writing implement to the other hand and now try beating your first score. Go on, give it your best shot!

How did you do the second time? Not so well I imagine?

Signature signing is a classic example of a habit formed over many years. In fact, for as long as we could read and write. In the same way we learnt to do this simple task with one hand we could have quite easily learnt with the other. So why didn't we? Well, as human beings, we tend to develop habits that are either taught (sometimes quite inadvertently) by parents, friends or work colleagues or else they are naturally acquired. And we tend to take the easy option because we are generally lazy creatures. Why learn to write with both hands if we can get away with one? From the moment we are born the habit forming process begins. How we talk, eat and walk; how we form attitudes and opinions; the things we like and dislike; how we work; how we sell and how we communicate.

Today, customers are information-conscious like never before but they, too, form habits and they all react differently to various stimuli. But I don't know one person who ever bought something because they understood every single technical detail of the product they were buying. Rather, they seek to buy because of a need. Of course, some people like to analyse and compare product features but ultimately they buy because they are value-conscious. If the benefits are perceived to outweigh cost then they invariably want what's on offer.

Product knowledge is something some sales people have in abundance. Certain individuals possess superlative prospecting or referral skills. Some could close almost any sale, whatever the objection.

But if it was all about what we know rather than what we do then why are most members of MENSA earning less than the average worker? Every successful business man and woman I know are fundamentally ordinary people yet still manage to achieve extraordinary things despite, sometimes, a lack of knowledge or technical ability. So why should this be?

Well, all - without exception - have a belief in their own ability and this is coupled with a focus and determination to succeed. Not surprisingly they seem to succeed most of the time.

Looking more closely at these individuals I realised that it wasn't necessarily about what they knew but about what they did. The action they took – daily, monthly, annually.

I discovered that we all have a potential we sometimes never even knew existed. Believe me, it's there - inside every person on earth.

Of course, I still advocate that we learn as much as we can, but selling a product or service is 75% the art of listening and salesmanship and only 25% product knowledge. Have the courage to tell people what you do – but not what you know. Have the courage to fail – because that's how you gain experience. Never, ever give up: remember your next meeting could result in a substantial sale.

The reason most people never unlock their true potential – the 'power within' – is because we find being mediocre easier than being successful. After all, it is easier to avoid taking action than to drop the excuse we have not to perform. Think of the person trying to win a one-hundred meter sprint with a ball and chain attached to one foot. It's almost impossible to win but yet most people would not want to be released from their constraint because it is more comfortable running at the back. To be a winner we have to accept the risk of defeat. Once we develop the courage to believe in ourselves then success comes much more easily. It is no longer a matter of chance but a matter of choice.

Have you ever been to a business meeting and listened intently to an excellent speaker who shared lots of good ideas? Did you come away thinking 'There were some really good ideas there: I'm gong to put them all into action tomorrow!' I suppose most of us have heard ourselves saying those words before now, but how often did we follow through on the commitment? If the answer is not very often, or never, then it begs the question 'Why are we wasting our time?'. In fact, why waste time and money on books, tapes and seminars if there is little chance we are going to try some of the ideas: ideas that we know will work for us and our business because they have worked for everyone else who found the time and made the effort?

I may appear to be a little sensitive on the subject but I make no apologies. The best idea in the world is as worthless as half an hour in the office with a cup of coffee and a crossword if it is not implemented. So before we start to invest time furthering our knowledge let's ask ourselves whether we are making the best use of what we already know. So may I suggest it is an good idea to start with a commitment to take action on every idea in this book?

By way of offering some assistance to that very important promise I ask you to attempt the practical exercises at the end of each chapter. They are there to ensure application of the simple and transferable ideas; ideas that have been instrumental to the success of not just my business but thousands of businesses over the years.

What great thing would you attempt if you could not fail? What is the greatest goal you could possibly imagine yourself achieving? I ask because it's important we know, right from the start, what our Primary Objective has to be; because without an ultimate or 'master' goal we will find the road to success very long and difficult indeed. Consider, for a moment, how your life could be if you achieve anything you wanted and think, only then, about the short, medium and longer term goals that will be needed to reach the target. For me, my Primary Objective is to spend an average of three days a week looking after a small, select, number of clients; to spend one day a week speaking, lecturing or writing and long weekends with my family. If my goal was simply to make a lot of money it is extremely unlikely I would fulfil my ambitions.

Although there will be an opportunity at the end of each chapter for you to implement any idea you wish to use in your business I also suggest you take a moment to think about anything in this book which particularly appeals. Think about the idea. Think about it in connection with your situation, your work, your lifestyle. Think about its value to you – how it could change and improve your life. Think about how you can apply it – and most importantly visualise yourself doing it and making it produce great results.

I hope to share many ideas that will have a positive impact on your business – but whether anything works is, ultimately, up to you. In order for us to produce a successful outcome we need two things: thought and action.

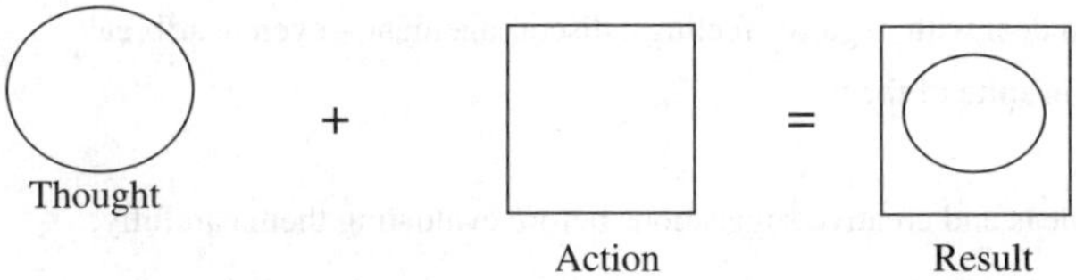

Occasionally, the process breaks down because something stops us taking action. It is something I refer to as INTERFERENCE and it can take many forms.

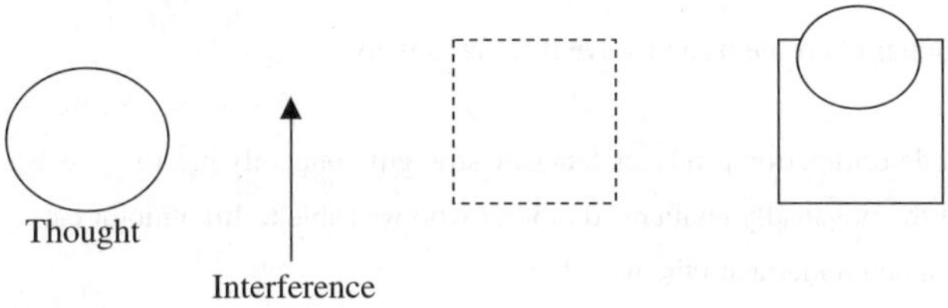

When we get distracted (as we inevitably do from time to time) a thought, however good, remains just that – a thought. So we need to be aware of the things that sometimes hold us back: compliance; unnecessary travelling; negative people; time-wasting in the office – and so on. Once we are aware of them we stand a much greater chance of eliminating them for good.

You've probably noticed that people seem to be generally divided into two main groups? In one group are winners; excited about what's happening in their lives. They are people who are usually optimistic, friendly and successful despite having, as we all do, problems from time to time. The people in the second group don't think of themselves as winners because they wait for things to happen to them – and then feel constantly betrayed because life never seems to move forward.

Every winner knows success does not come without its risks – and I would suggest it is the risk of failure (as much as the risk of success) that stops many people taking the vital step; a step that might lead them to their goal. Most successful, positive, action-orientated people have not reached life's pinnacle because they have unique talent or because they have specialist knowledge or training. The reason they have made it to the top of their profession or reached their goal is because they have learned to do four things:

1. They have learned to deal with negative feelings, discouragement – even heartbreak – and react positively in spite of them;

2. They listen to new ideas and creative suggestions before evaluating them carefully;

3. They spot opportunities and seize them courageously;

4. They welcome challenging problems and solve them creatively.

It is a known fact that great determination produces fantastic strength: one only has to consider the news article of the physically challenged mother who was able to lift a motor car in order to save her child trapped underneath the wheels.

Immersing yourself in positive thinking; mixing with people who are not constantly bemoaning their lack of success and taking action at every opportunity will eventually build such power into your thinking that it will be almost impossible to fail at anything.

Here's an idea I've used to great effect for many years. In fact, I should go so far as to say it has been one of the biggest contributing factors to the rapid business and financial success I have achieved in a relatively short space of time.

I call it Mindchangers.

Mindchangers are a series of statements – of no more than twenty words – which I write down and then review every day, without fail. What is significant about these simple statements, however, is that they are all written using very inspiring and positive language and in a way that would imply I have just fulfilled one of my goals. For example:

> "Paying for my new Mercedes in cash gave me the most fantastic feeling".

Simply writing down a list of objectives (some would call them goals) hardly inspires. It is the conscious mind which stores the images of goals created in this way; but there is only one problem. The conscious mind is prone to distraction so we are often sidetracked by interference and so we often miss out on achievement.

Whilst I do not profess to be a psychologist I do know that the sub-conscious mind is infinitely more powerful than the conscious mind. After all we walk, talk, breathe and recall certain information at will; without having to think about what we are doing. So let's imagine we could commit our goals, ambitions and dreams to our sub-conscious – what then? Well, Mindchangers are now used by most of the people I have ever worked with, or coached, and I have witnessed some incredible results.

The (Mercedes) Mindchanger mentioned above was actually one of my own written in 1996. I read the statement, along with sixty-two others, every day before I went to my office and in every case habits started to form, without me necessarily being aware of them. Remarkably I would find myself telephoning, without particular reason, the Mercedes garage and discussing the car I was going to purchase; describing it in detail. Actually, this happened regularly and yet, apart from a brief glance at my Mindchangers each morning, I hadn't really given much thought to the purchase of a Mercedes; especially knowing I was on a fifteen month waiting list. Every time I called the showroom I'd end up describing a different feature of the car or, strangely, going out that day and writing more business than normal. I'd obviously convinced myself I was going to purchase this car for cash. Then one day, out of the blue, I had a call. It was the Mercedes salesman with whom I had by now struck up a firm friendship. He told me that he had a cancelled order from the owner of a business who was in financial difficulty; but because I had so accurately described my 'dream' car and because it so closely matched the cancelled order vehicle he called me straight away to avoid the struggle of finding another prospective purchaser on his fifteen-month waiting list. Was it luck or, maybe, fate that contrived to ensure I achieved my goal? Eventually, I suppose, I would have taken delivery of a brand new sports car. But there is a big difference between those who wait for their boat to come in and those who swim out to meet it: and there is a big difference to the levels of success we will undoubtedly achieve by creating habits out of goals rather than listing objectives as distant dreams.

You can use your imagination, through the use of Mindchangers, to absolutely change your life, the lives of others and the world around you. I dare you to try it: you will be astounded at the results!

If, as I suspect, you are already sceptical then I would suggest you might struggle to get much from this book because it is designed to prompt positive action – now. So please suspend all cynicism and at least try. Read your statements every single day without fail. Remember: winners look to the future, not to the past. They understand that if we continue to get what we've been doing we'll continue to get what we've been getting. That is an absolute guarantee.

I would even go so far as to suggest you use Mindchangers to deal with any problems. For example:

> "The champagne tasted fantastic. I'm glad I rewarded myself for paying off my debts"

Although we will look more closely at Mindchangers in Chapter Four here's a great way to manage a problem. The trouble with problems, usually, is that they prompt some people to give up; surrendering to discouragement, depression, failure or defeat. Winners, on the other hand, manage whatever problems come up because there will always be obstacles along the way. With this in mind I encourage you to spot a worthwhile opportunity, prepare for any potential problems and then simply move ahead without delay. Great opportunities never last long!

Goals are key to success. Without them we would not have a 'track to run on' and would find any kind of achievement extraordinarily difficult.

Set low goals and you limit yourself to low achievement. Set high goals – even seemingly impossible ones – and you give yourself up to maximum energy, maximum creativity, maximum achievement and maximum reward.

Before we start planning our future successes as business people we must first plan our own lives. What do we truly want by way of a Primary Objective? To spend more time with our families; keep fit; start a college course; travel or retire early? Without knowing how our lives need to look in order to complete our journey how can we possibly go about setting goals for our businesses along the path of life?

When asking yourself what it is you really want, have the courage to set some stiff challenges. With a positive mental attitude – always – you will be amazed at what can be achieved.

If you ever find yourself thinking you can't do something, consider what you will achieve by at least trying to provide something a competitor does not; because if you can't do what somebody else can, you are simply denying yourself a chance to have whatever it is you want. The only reason we ever think we 'can't' is because of a lack of confidence in our own abilities. One common fear amongst sales professionals is that we find ourselves with a prospect or client who asks a technical question and we don't know the answer. So what? Will all be lost if we simply admit we don't know and refer the question to a colleague or look it up in a book? Of course not! In fact, relationships can be built on an honest answer; because honesty gains respect. Maybe it's a lack of confidence because of the fear of rejection? I accept it is easy to take a 'No' personally but, by reading this book, you'll find there are a number of ways to avoid rejection.

So what's the problem? There is always someone around to help. All we need to do is ask.

Once we find a way around potentially damaging negativity we start to build confidence and self-esteem. Our work then improves, our personal relationships get better and we feel healthier, more cheerful and far more resilient.

The self-confident person dares to be honest and open. This type of person accepts that they are a unique individual who reflects a basic integrity of character together with a clear knowledge and understanding of their business. It's extraordinary what we can create for ourselves without trying too hard.

If you are now thinking of time (or lack of it) or an excuse as to 'why not' then I would argue that, particularly if you are anything like every other person on this planet, you spend at least 30% of each day non-productively. This book is not about time management but it is about encouraging better use of our time. What would a 30% increase in productivity do for you if we could find a way to use time more productively and in a more balanced way? I use the word balance because a great number of people have spent years working sixteen hours a day; earned a 'million' but ended up in the divorce courts. I ask you to simply be aware of non-productive time and attempt to fill it with the implementation of an idea from this book, for example. What do you have to lose? Absolutely nothing!

Lets summarise our journey so far:

Understand Your Life Goals.

It's vital to understand what outcomes we are ultimately looking to achieve. Our Primary Objective should be the focus around which we create our other performance goals.

Develop Performance Goals

Once you know what you are trying to achieve consider the things you need to do to help achieve the outcome. Commit your goals to your sub-conscious by using 'Mindchangers'.

React Positively to Fear

As the great Mehdi Fakharadzeh says in his book 'Nothing Is Impossible' our limits are set only by ourselves. Why not approach life and business with total confidence? It's so much more fun and rewarding!

Be Aware of Interference

The effective use of time and the elimination of negative influences. Learn to say 'No'.

Measure Performance

Keep records, if you can, of the improvement in results – and develop a reward system. Use the assessment checklist at the end of this chapter to help.

Maintain Balance

We might end up wealthier in ten years time but how successful would we have been if we had lived those years like a pauper?. Most of us die before we ever get that 'minute to ourselves'. So don't let yourself say "Life won't always be this busy".

Embrace Change

If changes are needed take positive action. Taking the first steps does not necessarily involve a change of strategy: it's about a change of heart.

Quotes

"Great people are just ordinary people with an extraordinary amount of determination."

"The best partnerships do not come from a 50/50 effort. They are because the effort is 100% both ways; unconditionally."

"Children don't spell LOVE, L-O-V-E: They spell LOVE, T-I-M-E!"

"Don't concentrate on giving your children what you didn't have as a child yourself: concentrate on giving them what you did get."

"It always seems impossible – until it is done."

"It is a funny thing about life: if you refuse to accept anything but the best, you very often get it."

"Destiny is not a matter of chance, it is a matter of choice."

TAKING ACTION

At the beginning of this chapter you'll remember I made mention of the fact that putting things into action was vital. So, before you move onto the next I ask you to attempt the following exercises. Without a commitment – whether you succeed or fail is immaterial at this stage – I regret to say you may well have spent money on this book quite unnecessarily. So, please, give them a go…….

1. Write down your Primary Objective (your ultimate life goal).
2. Write down a list of your goals – short, medium and long-term.,
3. Commit at least 10 of these goals to Mindchanger cards and read them briefly each day. Ideally, create one Mindchanger for <u>every</u> goal.
4. Copy the following onto a sheet of paper and score yourself based on where you are right now. 1 is low, 10 is high. We'll review your progress later in the book:

a. Self Confidence
b. Personal Ambitions
c. Adapting to change
d. Persistence
e. Taking Action
f. Order and Organisation
g. Communication (with others)
h. Personal Appearance
i Plans and Planning
j. Time Management
k. Daily activity awareness
l. Focus
m. Dealing with Problems
n. Happiness and Personal Contentment
o. Physical condition/achievement
p. Sales

WARNING Do not procrastinate: do these exercises before you move to Chapter 2.

CHAPTER TWO – OPENING THE DOOR

First impressions have little to do with our appearance; what we say or even what we do when we meet a client or prospect. The process starts the first time someone hears about us so we need that impression to be positive. The best way to achieve this is to be publicly endorsed by someone else. That is why the building of a network of clients and professional contacts is so vital to good quality personal recommendations. It may seem obvious but we want prospects (a properly qualified client introduction) and not a suspect – which is merely a name and telephone number.

The creation of a simple marketing 'engine' makes things so much easier and it is incredibly easy to create. There are two groups I specifically target to help me with my business: my best clients (say, the top 20% based on net wealth or income) and other professionals who are what I would call 'Centres of Influence' because they have a trusted relationship with clients of their own.

As a general rule business owners know other business owners and wealthy people know other wealthy people so why not start by arranging meetings with your best clients – and asking them for their help in building your business. Such help means you can spend 80% of your time looking after them and 20% of your time looking for new clients; rather than the other way around. What is (pleasantly) surprising is that most human beings, if asked, normally respond positively to requests for assistance: yet we rarely take the time to ask. If we provide a good, reliable, honest and trustworthy service why shouldn't we expect a little in return; particularly if we put a proposal to our clients in this way? The establishment of several trusted advocates who can reinforce the image we are trying to create will create what we all know as effective branding. For our part, however, we must consistently deliver in terms of professionalism; from logos and stationory to advertising and marketing.

But how do we get the appointment once we have identified those who can help build our business?

GETTING THE APPOINTMENT

Getting the appointment should actually be easy – because our prospect will hopefully have come from a strong personal recommendation.

If you absolutely must cold-call then I suggest the use of something I call the Dynamic 'Phone Path. It is a 'system' I used successfully in the early days and the results were staggering compared to the rather feeble and nervous efforts I made on the telephone when I first started out. It has also worked for many other advisers since I was first introduced to it by my business 'coach' and mentor Glen McCoy.

DYNAMIC 'PHONE PATH

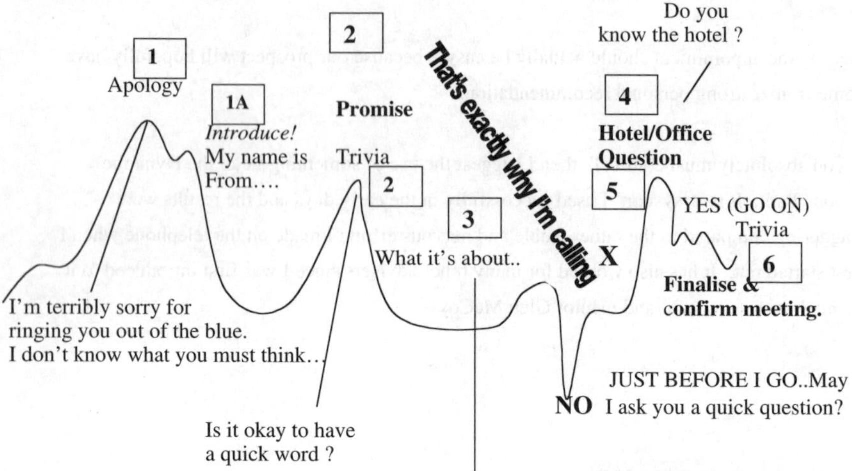

1 Bills
2 Business loans
3 Credit cards
4 Personal Mortgages
5 Capital

Notes…

1. Get to 3 ASAP!

2. Give a BENEFIT of getting together

Strategic Words

I am a business development specialist helping business owners create powerful strategies to increase their bottom lines. The help I give is much more than financial planning.

I offer an initial complementary business brain storm. Would that be of value?

THE DYNAMIC 'PHONE PATH

The whole concept of the Dynamic 'Phone Path is to make it as easy as possible, during a telephone call, to get a prospective client to say 'yes' to an initial meeting. In other words, it is an easy-to-apply approach to prospecting.

To start with, an apology is always very effective because it is a polite and caring way to begin a conversation. This is followed by the introduction. The 'promise' comes next which reads something like "I've recently taken on (name of individual) as a client and your name came up in conversation; hence the promise to call….!"

The word 'promise' is key because it will get our prospect thinking 'this adviser keeps his/her promises'. Trust is therefore easier to establish.

Next, asking for permission to have a conversation is a courtesy demonstrating respect and an acknowledgement that the call is unsolicited.

The prospect will almost certainly ask what the purpose of the call is and so an appropriate response is required to generate interest. The use of strategic words, as detailed within the Dynamic Phone Path model, will help to move the conversation to the next stage. However it may be that, at this point, an 'objection' is encountered. A comment such as "You're not calling to sell me something are you?" or It's not life insurance is it?" can be followed with the reply "That's exactly why I'm calling. Although I do help people plan to meet their family protection needs I actually spend most of my time…." and then the conversation can develop around a subject that may be of more interest to the prospect.

When studying the suggested model you will notice the 'path' is never a straight one: it rises and falls in the same way that your prospect reacts emotionally and verbally to the things they hear. If, at stage three, the individual is receptive to a meeting move straight to stage four and agree a time and place to meet. I always think a hotel is best because it rids both prospect and adviser of any potential distractions from their office or home environment.

But, as we know, a 'No' or 'Not interested' can be introduced by our prospect at this stage. This is, on occasions, inevitable and can never be totally avoided – even with the Dynamic Phone Path as a 'track to run on'.

Whilst we might ordinarily think that this is now the time to accept this almost final request to take the conversation no further I would suggest this is the time to introduce "Just before I go…may I ask you a quick question?" I must admit, I can't remember anyone ever saying "No" when I've put this to them at the 'end' of the conversation. "Do you currently get a discount on your household bills?/Do you have a *self-cancelling business overdraft?/Do you have…." The question could be anything at all – as long as it provokes interest and creates a desire to know more. "What do you mean, a self-cancelling overdraft?" asks the prospect. "Well, if you're free on Tuesday we could meet and I'll show you exactly what I mean. Do you know the ABC hotel?"

Usually I end the conversation with the usual pleasantries or trivia and then confirm the meeting.

**In case you were wondering, a Self Cancelling Overdraft is a banking facility that is repaid from the proceeds of a life assurance policy on the death or disability of the business owner.*

So how does the script look in detail?

THE DYNAMIC 'PHONE PATH SCRIPT

Mr……I'm terribly sorry to call you out of the blue like this – I don't usually make a professional habit of it. My name is …….. from ……… Is it alright to talk for a moment?

*I've recently taken on………… as a client and your name came up in conversation a couple of times….hence the promise to call…..and offer you my help, since I make it a professional business practice to work with the friends and families of my clients before anyone else.

Do you know the ……. hotel?
May I suggest we meet at the …….so that I may have the opportunity on sharing some similar ideas with yourself? What time of the day suits you best?
If there is an objection, agree (That is exactly why I am calling…..) and proceed to "Just before I go….."
If 'Yes', gain appointment and confirm.

If 'No', "Just before I go.....May I ask you a quick question?
You must pay a lot of money out in bills....? If it were possible to reduce those bills in some way would that be of value to you....?"

If 'Yes', gain appointment and confirm.

*At this point you may like to vary the 'script' depending on how the telephone conversation has come about. The one I've suggested would be best used following a direct introduction (a personal recommendation) but "The reason for the call is......" could be best for an 'orphan' client and "I'm calling to ....." for a small business.

Try it for yourself....it does work! But don't be afraid to fail with an approach to any client or customer. After all, we have all failed at just about everything we have ever attempted for the first time: walking, swimming, writing, speaking. I would suggest that instead of worrying about failure we should be worrying about the chances we miss when we don't even try!

If you absolutely detest telephone 'prospecting, ' here's an idea that will eliminate the fear. Forever. It's called a "Hello" call and is not, in any way, sales orientated. Your purpose is simply to call an existing client to discuss anything you may feel like mentioning (birthday; anniversary; enquiring after the family) and nothing more.

What comes from an 'Hello' call? Well, maybe nothing at all – except a delighted client who has never experienced such attention from someone who, works in a profession full of people who only ever contact their clients when they have something to sell. Or, it may just prompt your client to say, Oh, I'm glad you telephoned. I'd like to talk to you about....."

In either instance you will never be rejected, so it's a great way of breaking up a telephone session and feeling great about yourself at the same time; which inevitably puts you in a better frame of mind for the next call.

THE FIRST MEETING

As we have already discussed, first impressions are everything. But so are, what I call, second impressions. Fail to create a clean, professional, image and you will undoubtedly struggle to win your client's trust and confidence.

It should go without saying that 'Golden Rule Number One' is to be punctual; yet so few sales people get this simple courtesy mastered. Usually, the advisers who are always late simply have a poor time management system; probably because they aren't allowing enough time for travelling or have not planned their workload properly. This can be easily corrected by following the guidance notes in the Chapter 4 of this book.

Even if we do get to our client on time we need to appear smart and well groomed. I despair of the advisers who smell of alcohol, tobacco or - worst of all - body odour. Turning up in an ill-fitting suit or with dirty shoes (or both) sends out completely the wrong message. I appreciate that a new wardrobe of clothes might be a bit extreme and beyond the financial scope of some, but one or two clean smart outfits will give our clients more confidence in our abilities as sales professionals.

Another thing often overlooked is the use of a nice writing implement. No client I know - especially the Chief Executive of a large company - is going to be terribly impressed if we were to suddenly produce a disposable pen from our pocket in order to take notes or complete an application form. Again, I'm not suggesting a huge investment in such an accessory but something that looks reasonably decent will impress.

There are many parts to building good impressions. Double check you are up to scratch by looking in the mirror before leaving for an appointment and ask yourself the question 'Would I buy from me?' If the answer is 'No' then I suggest some corrective action is necessary.

Nothing will be achieved by blitzing our prospect with the benefit of our technical knowledge, however good. Neither is there anything to be gained by going straight into a perfectly-rehearsed sales script. The quickest and most effective way of establishing trust (the most fundamental of all building blocks in any relationship) is to spend time selling yourself. I always, without fail, spend five or ten minutes sharing information on my business: what we do, our philosophies, our working practices. During my introduction I explain how we differ from other firms of advisers and talking about what makes us unique. The reason for this is simple: firstly I want to build rapport and then I want my clients to like and trust me. I want them to have confidence in my commitment and ability to serve them well. Secondly I want to be sure I sell value, not price. Selling price is the certain way to business failure because you can be sure that if you don't already work in a business sector where the same product can be obtained at the same price almost anywhere else then someone will always find a way to undercut you. So I talk about what else I can bring to the client; over and above the creation of a sound financial portfolio designed to create wealth.

Once I have handed over my Business Card and Terms of Business (in the UK this is a simple document designed to confirm the status of the adviser – whether 'tied' or independent) I will say the following:

"Mr/s Prospect, do you mind if I just spend five or ten minutes telling you a little about me and my business? Thank you......

I have been in the insurance business for thirteen years; the last five running my own private practice. The business was built on some key principles; not least that we look to build long term relationships with our clients. We believe this is fundamental to the financial planning process because continuity of advice and service is - we have found through the questionnaires we send to our clients - the most important thing people look for in a relationship with a professional adviser.

We are one of, if not the only, business of our kind to have a written Client Service Charter which outlines the way we go about building those relationships. Every client is treated in an honest, ethical and professional manner; we respond to telephone calls and letters within given time frames or we pay a financial penalty to a charity of your choice. Fortunately, we don't get caught out too often but when we do you can be sure we will be striving to ensure the same mistake never happens again.

Most significantly of all we work with a number of business partners; for example Solicitors, Accountants, Stockbrokers, Mortgage Brokers and General Insurance Brokers. This allows you to access a full range of services with one telephone call to us. If you have your own family Solicitor or Accountant then we'd be only too pleased to work with them. But for those people who don't, I'm sure you can see the benefit of accessing all the services you will might need, from time to time, under one roof? The more services you use, the greater the discounts – because we can use our 'buying power' as a company to negotiate on your behalf. So, for example, if you arrange your mortgage through us we can recommend the services of a Solicitor with whom we have negotiated a discounted fee for the legal work; often amounting to a significant saving. In addition, we can offer discounted home insurance; saving you more money. Our philosophy is we'd rather have seventy percent of all your business than one hundred percent of nothing.

I have a number of other ideas that could save you considerable amounts of money. If you can just tell me a little about you I'll pick up on this again. Is that OK?"

It is important to get your prospect saying 'Yes' right from the start. Maybe a little compliment here or a word of sympathy, if necessary, there. Does your prospect want to save time? Yes. Does your prospect want to save money? Yes. Does your prospect want to provide for his/her financial future? Yes.

Consider, for a moment, the introductory 'script' I use with my prospects. I believe it encapsulates everything I want, and need, to say at this early stage in the relationship. I mention, openly, the things they will undoubtedly want from an adviser – trust, honesty, professionalism and a long-term relationship. The idea that we are so confident in our ability to deliver good service that we will pay a fine to charity if we let our client down does get results. I freely admit we do make mistakes occasionally (no-one can ever be perfect) but this honesty only serves to endorse what I say about our commitment to building trust.

Then, of course, my prospective clients get to find out that they have just met the one adviser who is committed to saving them money; someone who is helping them invest for the future. Think of the number of clients who would happily recommend to friends, relatives and business colleagues if we were able to provide a financial plan at no or little cost? I have, on many an occasion, had clients open their personal telephone book and offer me the entire list of names and numbers.

Finally, they are reassured at knowing you are the person who, following a telephone call, will be on hand to deal with all their financial affairs. I'm not saying I would personally handle their tax returns nor the legal formalities of buying a house but, by sub-contracting the work to other professionals I trust, I retain complete control of the client. However, the most important bit of all is that we now have a client who will probably need to contact us several times a year. That's several more opportunities to have a conversation and several more personal recommendations. In short, your clients 'service' themselves.

When the clients start to talk about themselves I usually just jot down notes on a piece of paper. I find that few people I have only just met feel comfortable with a formal question and answer session in order to get a 'Fact Find' completed. It's also amazing how much more information you can gather if you keep things informal. Ask lots of 'open' questions (questions that need more of an answer than just 'yes' or 'no') such as 'How do you feel about ……?' or 'What do you think of …..?' Listening is very important at this stage.

After I have all the basic information I remind them of my promise to talk about other money saving ideas; ideas which actually lend themselves well to the completion of the Fact Find. So I will ask which credit card(s) they use; whom their mortgage and home insurance is with; what existing policies they have; whether they pay bank charges; how much they paid in legal and accountancy fees last year and whether they have made a Will.

There is, more often than not, considerable potential to save large sums of money – particularly if you have strategic alliances with other advisers who can help you put a discounted portfolio together.

Some advisers baulk at the suggestion they should 'waste' time by talking about saving money on credit cards when there is 'nothing in it' for them - but I beg to differ. Firstly, referring them to a local bank manager with whom you have negotiated a special rate on savings accounts or credit cards - or just providing an application form for completion - takes no time at all. It's all part of value-added service. If we don't compete on service then our businesses are almost certainly doomed to failure because, in an ever more competitive environment, we won't always be able to compete on price alone.

ASKING FOR PERSONAL INTRODUCTIONS

If we approach this in the right way there is nothing to stop us asking for personal introductions at the first meeting, irrespective of whether your prospects are likely to become clients or not. The reason? You will be asking them whether they know anyone else who would be interested in saving money and that always prompts a positive response. The reason I ask in this way is because I am all too aware of what a client is really thinking when I have asked, in the past, 'Is there anyone else you know who you feel would benefit from my services?' Roughly translated, they think they are being asked 'Do you know anyone else to whom I can sell something?' and it is for this reason prospects say things like 'I can't really think of anyone' or 'Everyone I know has got their own adviser'. It's not that they don't trust you – they just want to avoid committing their best friend to spending money on the products you are selling.

However, if we sell value - not price - they'll soon want to introduce us to everyone they know.

But let's say for a moment it really is difficult asking the all-important question; the answer to which could be the difference between a good week and a bad week. I would suggest that if it is just not your style to ask for a personal introduction then don't; at least not initially anyway. I have always held a view that the acid test of a great client-adviser relationship is the fact that we can talk to our clients like we talk to, say, one of our own family.

If we are still addressing most of our clients as 'Mr' or 'Mrs' after knowing them for several months I suggest we have a problem. Occasionally, when I need a boost of confidence by generating some new business I'll ring one or two of my best clients and say something like

"Hello". And, after the usual pleasantries, say "I've just noticed from my file that I've never had any personal recommendations from you. You're the only one I've met in the last (period of time) that hasn't introduced me to someone else – what's going on?"

Admittedly I will have a chuckle about it so my client isn't offended by the rather direct approach but it really is like that when I speak to them. But why shouldn't it be? After all, I've provided an excellent service; I'm honest, trustworthy and always put my clients best interests first. Therefore I don't think anyone could forgive me for almost expecting a personal introduction – or several. That is not to say I'm arrogant about it: I just want to do my best for as many people as possible. If there are to be other nine year olds left without a father, as I was, I don't want the family to struggle financially just because I didn't do my job properly. So I'm certainly not going to quit just because my client hasn't offered me twenty names on a plate.

And another thing. When was the last time you were given a really hard time by a prospect? Most prospects who say 'No' to an approach usually add a 'Thank You' and are mostly very pleasant. Interestingly, the more corporate the client the nicer the rejection: I've had some lovely rejections down the years!

But therein lies the rub; every rejection takes us one step closer to our next client. And rejection – which is never personal anyway – is a necessary (and unavoidable) part of what we do. If we can't accept it we can forget about making it to the top of our profession. Resilience and determination is what separates the best from the mediocre.

Quotes

"We can achieve everything we want to achieve if only we have the courage to believe we can achieve it."

"We should stop worrying about failure and worry about the opportunities we miss when we don't even try."

"A big business is a small business that did well."

"Don't be afraid to fail with an approach to any client or customer. After all, we have all failed at just about everything we have ever attempted: swimming; riding a bicycle; writing; speaking. What's so different now?"

"Obstacles are the things you see when you fail to focus on your goals."

"Accept the challenges so that you may feel the exhilaration of victory."

"Genius is one percent inspiration and ninety-nine percent perspiration."

TAKING ACTION

1. If you don't already have one: design an introductory script which you will use at every first meeting. Learn it 'by heart'.

2. As soon as you can, buy yourself a new business outfit.

3. Make 10 calls using the Dynamic Phone Path and make every third call a 'Hello' call.

4. Find out the best credit card, loan and mortgage deals available and carry a few application forms with you. Hand them to your clients, where appropriate. Better still, build relationships with a bank manager, lawyer, accountant and the other professionals who could add value by offering discounts on their services, without committing you to any work.

5. Call your top 20 clients and ask them to help you build your business by introducing you to other people like them.

CHAPTER THREE – KEEPING IT SIMPLE

When I started my career I wondered how well suited I was for the job. People immediately told me I was too young and I questioned whether I was convincing enough or that I had 'what it took' to be a success. But I soon came to realise that it is honesty, ability, willingness to learn and perseverance that would determine the level of my success; nothing else. Our business is not about the products we sell but about the people we are. Clients buy the individual first; concept and ideas second and any product as a natural consequence of that process. Of course, ignoring these basic standards may still get us a sale but the relationship with a prospective client is unlikely to develop. Lasting relationships require honesty and sincerity. Generally, clients really don't care how many options or benefits a policy has; they want to know, for example, what benefits they are getting for their investment. We don't get paid by the hour but for the value we bring to an hour. Quoting percentages and estimated rates of growth might be something we are obliged to do as part of a professional code of conduct but it is not what move people to action.

For these reasons it nearly always works best to convey things simply. Equally, trying to impress your client with how smart you are will generally not establish trust nor help the relationship building process. After all, if your client thought you were stupid they wouldn't be talking to you. Education – and giving a client the benefit of that knowledge – is, of course, important but it is only half the equation. Transferring knowledge and ideas into concepts that clients can easily understand is far more important.

CONCEPT SELLING

It doesn't matter whether we are trying to sell to the most financially naïve individual or to a rocket scientist, there are still some basics to cover.

In the days when I was in management I remember visiting a client with one of my more experienced advisers. The first meeting had gone well and now he was back, with me an on-looker from the corner of his client's living room, to 'make the sale'. In fact, we were there to present solutions for four identified needs; there was a clear requirement to address their life cover, income protection, pension and private medical insurance needs. The solutions to his client's problems were sound and the premiums fitted comfortably within the stated budget. What could possibly go wrong? It was a formality - or so my agent thought.

What he failed to realise was that his client was not in the least bit technically minded nor did she, in fact, want to know about every last detail on the quotation or the vast array of paperwork that followed. She simply wanted to know what most of us want to know: what was being recommended (product); what did it do (benefits) and how much would it cost (premium)?

Not picking this up, the adviser proceeded to bombard the poor woman with technical detail like you wouldn't believe. Were his efforts compliant? Certainly. But were they effective? Not at all.

Having sat back in his chair, confident of getting his client's agreement following his twenty-five-minute-client-brain-washing-session my adviser was dumb-struck when his client suggested that she needed time to think about his recommendations.

At that point, not wanting to see a grown man cry, I leaned forward and asked the lady whether I could simply summarise. She seemed almost relieved: so I proceeded to write - on a single sheet of paper - what she was being asked to invest in; what was being recommended and the basic benefit each plan provided. The piece of paper was divided into twelve equal segments, four rows of three, and each box containing a word or number. Within five minutes we were completing the application forms.

This summary report, as I refer to it, is now a regular feature at my presentation meetings. I sell the concept first; the technical details second.

Of course I am not suggesting for a moment that we do not comply with our obligations to provide full product and commission disclosure or explain the quotation in detail. But there is nothing to stop us explaining the benefits behind our recommendations before we proceed to the more technical aspects. A single sheet of paper, set out in the way I have described above, is an extremely effective way to help our clients understand the rationale behind a recommendation - and it is this that they buy. If the recommendation, however simple, makes sense and clearly fits their need and budget then there are not likely to be any objections.

I am a great believer in keeping things simple for a client. Even those who want considerable amounts of detail and technical information still want the thinking behind the advice presented in a straight-forward way.

There are many other conceptual ideas I use when I need to help a client see how important it is to take positive action; irrespective of whether this results in a sale.

One of the other ideas I use is something I call the 'Two Jobs' presentation. Lets assume for a moment our client currently enjoys a salary of £29,000 ($42,500) per annum and drives a company car. I will start by taking him back to the time they were first interviewed, and accepted, for the job that currently provides these benefits. I would say something like 'When you first took your job you were offered £29,000 ($42,500) a year and a company car. Presumably you are still quite happy with the package that you received from your employer today? What I would like you to imagine now is that I am the same person who interviewed you for the job – except on this occasion I am going to offer you £28,000 ($40,800) a year and the same company car. But I'm also going to provide Income Protection, which ensures up to 50% of your salary will continue to be paid to you in the event of accident, sickness or long-term illness; Death-in-Service cover, which will ensure your family will receive a lump sum equal to three times your annual salary in the event of your demise. You'll also receive a lump sum in the event of diagnosis of cancer, heart attack, stroke or a number of other serious illnesses. In addition to those benefits your employer would make a contribution to a pension plan in your name and you would also be offered private medical insurance for you and your family. Let me ask: would you have taken this job if it had been offered? And even now, which of the two jobs do you consider to be more attractive?'

THE TWO JOBS CONCEPT

JOB A	JOB B
• £29,000 pa	• £28,000 pa
• Company car	• Income Protection (50% of salary)
	• Death in Service (3 x salary)
	• Critical Illness (2 x salary)
	• Personal Pension
	• Private Medical Insurance
	• Company Car

In twelve years I have never yet come across a client who has told me that the first of the two job offers seemed to be worth far more than the latter. Instead all, without exception, point to the 'second' job offer and make the type of comments which only goes to prove that the benefits - many of which would provide for their family - significantly outweigh the cost. Bear in mind, too, that most people realise additional taxes will need to be paid on the higher salary option so the alternative job offer appears much better value for money. I would suggest this is an excellent sales 'aid,' when presenting several solutions to either an existing or prospective client because it is in a form which they can grasp far more easily.

STRESS MANAGEMENT

Plan your day the night before so that you will start the day feeling organised and in control. Prioritise and learn how to delegate: you are not the only person who can do the job. Make sure you take time to explain exactly what is required for the person to whom you are delegating.

Be positive! Having a laugh helps you to detach from your problems and gives you a fresh perspective. It also relaxes muscles, eases tiredness and boosts circulation. Stress-free people are optimists. If you feel positive and upbeat, you will radiate this to other people and attract the same attitude. Take one job at a time, however quick or easy it seems. Do lots of jobs quickly and you are more likely to need to do some of them again. Don't put things off – procrastinating will give you higher stress levels than just dealing with situations as they arise. Don't allow domestic tasks to dominate your life. Life is too short to spend pre-occupied with mundane chores.

Sometimes imagining the worst case scenario can help you see your problems are not as bad as you think: consider the many people who are in a more unfortunate position and use this as a foundation to build a positive mental attitude. Imagine what advice you would give a friend in the same situation. It is often easier to solve a dilemma for someone else.

In summary, stress is a response that comes from within ourselves, rather than from outside factors such as work. It is important to remember that we can choose whether to continue or to stop whatever it is that is causing the problem.

SOME OTHER CONCEPTUAL IDEAS

1. Which Do You Insure?

Monthly Pay Cheque

I personally find it remarkable that we, as human beings, are quick to insure material items in our lives such as cars, audio and television equipment and the homes in which we live. But how many of us insure the pay cheques that we receive each month? I have heard many financial services professionals use the question 'If you had a machine in your cellar that each time you turned the handle produced £500 (£750) in cash would you insure it against breakage or malfunction?' The answer, of course, is 'Yes'. Isn't that a bit like insuring your pay cheque with the amount produced relative to earnings? Personally I like to show a few simple diagrams on a piece of paper, like the ones above, because most people react to visual stimulus rather than a spoken word.

2. **Commission & Fees**

Whether we charge fees or take commission we need to consider how we are going to deal with this issue, if necessary.

Commission earnings are becoming an ever more contentious issue but any problems that arise generally come about because we are not prepared for the questions a client may ask. It is all too easy for a client to assume that commission (turnover) is profit. As we know, however, there are many costs to consider such as insurance, secretarial support, heat, light and our most valuable asset – time.

There will, of course, be occasions when it is difficult to justify a large commission payment when the work undertaken has been relatively straightforward. But if you are prepared to share my philosophy that 'what goes around comes around' explain to a client that with, such a work ethic, there will be times when a considerable amount of work will be undertaken with little or no remuneration. To my mind it is a fair way of working and the vast majority of clients will accept this without condition. If we agree the parameters within which we work, right at the outset, there will not be so many last-minute issues to deal with at the point of sale.

3. **Self Cancelling Loans and Overdrafts**

Referring back to the Dynamic Phone Path ask your corporate client whether they have a self-cancelling loan or overdraft. When they say 'No' you can advise them that for a fractional increase in the cost of their loan or rate charged on their overdraft you can see to it that the company's debts are wiped out in the event of death, disability or critical illness of a key person in the company; otherwise known as Key Person Assurance.

4. **Puppet on a String**

Good for Key Person Assurance or Shareholder Protection. Draw a puppet on a string. Ask the questions 'Mr/s Prospect, if you ran a puppet show who would you insure – the puppet or the person who pulls the strings?

5. **Where on the Line?**

X |————————————————————| Y

(Min premium) (Max premium)

You have established that the minimum investment amount for the policy you are recommending is 'X' per month and that 'Y' is the maximum. Ask your prospect or client to indicate where on the line they would be comfortable investing each month.

Remember: The premium chosen (whatever it is) is only a small fraction of the size of the problem.

6. **Cycling up the Hill**

The analogy of cycling up a hill; the steepness of which becomes more pronounced the longer our client leaves financial planning, is one that is well known.

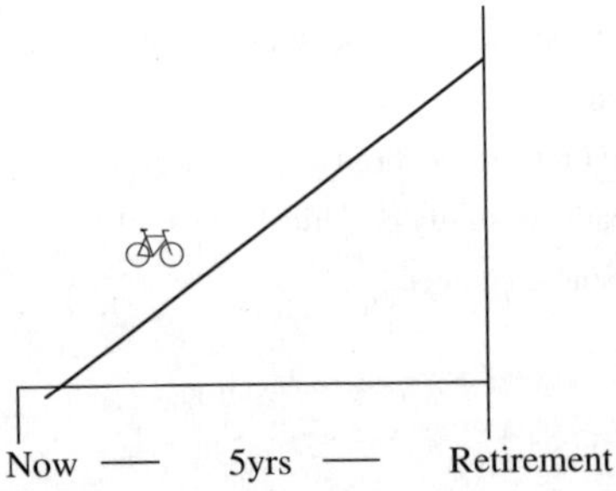

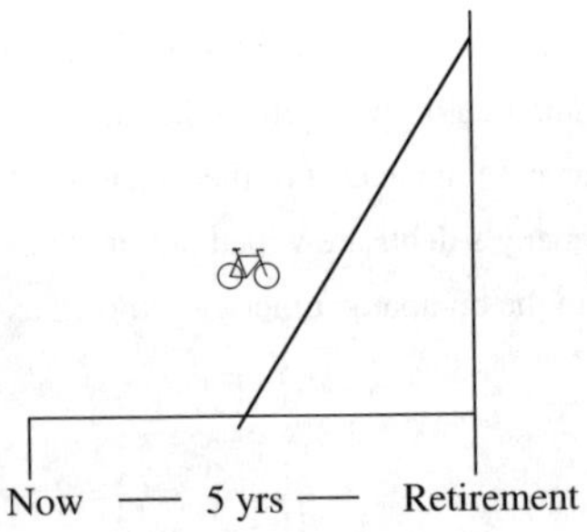

How often though do we stop to think about our own hill? I'm not necessarily talking about a sound financial plan for ourselves (although I've never quite understood why some sales people have never purchased their own products) but I am questioning why we make life so difficult for ourselves on occasions; leaving jobs to the last moment; avoiding confrontations; not being 'there' for our children whilst they were growing up. Leave it all too late and the hill can sometimes be too steep to climb.

The same applies to our businesses. We want to increase our productivity but somehow expect this to miraculously materialise with the minimum of effort. If there are, on average, two (domestic) client meetings in our diary each week then we'd need a considerable amount of luck to survive financially; never mind qualify for conventions and awards or to have the time to spend doing the things we enjoy doing. With an average of five client appointments we might just be making a living and with ten, enough to be considered reasonably successful.

But is it really just about working harder or is it about working smarter? If you are just starting out then you are probably concentrating on the former and with an established practice, the latter. Personally, I think a bit of both is required. Most of us, though, barely survive; marking time until the weekend when we can't wait to get home.

So how can we stop the hill getting steeper? I suggest a number of things:

- Eliminate unnecessary time in the office.
- Carefully plan travel routes, leaving enough time between appointments. Better still, ask your clients to visit you and offer some kind of incentive, if it helps eliminate non productive time.
- Avoid taking unnecessary calls. Ask staff or colleagues to properly identify each caller and the purpose of the call.
- Avoid extended lunch hours and attending to personal matters in working time.
- Eliminate coffee breaks and crosswords from your daily routine.
- Move your desk away from any disruptive or negative influences. Work from home if necessary.
- Don't dodge responsibilities.

7. **The 10% Account**.

This is a really simple, but effective, discipline which I would suggest everyone uses, if possible. Whatever we earn in salary, commission or fees set ourselves a target of saving 10% in a high-interest-bearing account; thus creating a fund we can then call on in the future. Quite apart from being a very effective savings idea this strategy should also provide the business owner with a possible exit strategy or, at worst, some capital value.

8. **Meeting Agenda**.

Why not consider visiting every client with a simple agenda in order to communicate, the financial planning process effectively? All too often financial professionals fall into the trap of 'making the easy sale' on the basis that a particular product is what our client appears to want. So why not write, or type, the words Short Term, Medium Term and Long Term onto a piece of paper and use this as an agenda; explaining that an effective financial plan can only be achieved by following a 'blue print?'. Such a simple concept is easy to understand and mostly ensures a balanced and strategic approach.

Remember, keep things simple but don't lose sight of the fact that time is money and on every occasion we procrastinate, fail to delegate or act decisively we are depriving ourselves of many of the great opportunities in life and business.

Quotes

“Anyone who doesn’t believe in life insurance deserves to die at least once without it.”

“We are the professionals who, when tragdegy strikes, walk in the front door with the money when everyone else is walking out of the back door with the money.”

“Nothing in the world can take the place of persistence. Talent will not; nothing is more common than unsuccessful men with talent. Genius will not; unrewarded genius” is almost a proverb. Education will not; the world is full of educated derelicts. Persistence and determination alone are omnipotent”.

(For clients who believe they cannot afford to pay the premiums) “If money is an issue, I’ll pay the premiums and your beneficiaries can pay me back out of the proceeds of the policy. If I’d do it for your family, why wouldn’t you?”

(To the business owner who does not value insurance; saying investment in his own business is better than wasting money on insurance) “That’s fine, but which would you rather give up to pay for the taxes and other charges when you die – your best investment or your worst investment?”

“ The highest reward for a person’s toil is not what thay get for it, but what they become by it”.

“ The different between ordinary and extraordinary is that little extra”.

TAKING ACTION

1. Try something really simple to help the habit forming process. Use the following grid to confirm that you are taking care of the necessary disciplines in your business each day. The items to be listed are those which require daily attention; such as writing a pre-determined level of business, making telephone calls, spending time with the family, exercise, strategic planning or anything else that needs to be included. Numbers one to seven correspond with the days of the week. Simply tick (check) to confirm the job has been done. There is a space for comments, if this is needed, but the most important thing is to ensure that, each and every day, positive action is being taken across all important business and personal disciplines. Remember any regular action that spans 28 days becomes a habit.

Item	1	2	3	4	5	6	7	Comments?

CHAPTER FOUR – PREPARE FOR ASTOUNDING SUCCESS

There is no doubt that good preparation is vital if we are to build firm foundations for a successful business.

If we are going to set goals then they must be inspirational and motivational. There is little point in creating a list of objectives if we do not have the commitment or determination to make them happen. But, as we know, that's easier said than done.

The Mindchanger idea is one that has been successfully adopted by thousands of people, with outstanding results. I must admit to being somewhat sceptical when I was first encouraged to use Mindchangers to help me achieve my goals but I was prepared to try it on the basis that we are 'guaranteed to miss 100% of the shots we don't take in life'. I originally put together fifty-eight statements which I then carried in my business diary and also had on my refrigerator at home. Following instructions, I reviewed my Mindchanger statements every day – for no more than five minutes – and then didn't think about them until I reviewed them again the following day. And so it went on – for several months.

After about six weeks I remember thinking I was wasting my time and that perhaps I should move onto another idea. But around the same time I also became aware I was going about my life and business activities in a different way. I was thinking differently, acting differently and behaving differently. Without being consciously aware of it I was doing and saying things which, looking back, were closely linked to the Mindchanger (goals) I had committed to paper.

Listed below are some of the Mindchangers I put together in the early days:

> Now I realise the importance of being a winner.
> My 'needing to win' thinking is taking me to the
> heights that most people only dream about…..

‘Yes!’
The word they use when I ask for introductions to others.

I love prospecting in the corporate/business market.

Main Platform speaker at Million Dollar Round Table. Who would have thought that two years ago?

After the incredible success of my first book I am now being commissioned to write two more.

The Forte Group is now so well known and successful that I have got some extremely high profile people trying to buy in.

Less and less is much, much more.

People seek me out to ask how I do what I do. I love sharing good ideas and I have no problem in doing that since I have more than I will ever need in my lifetime.

These were some of the Mindchangers that inspired me to achieve a level of success and experience that I could pass onto others, since I had always liked the idea of public speaking. So, without really giving it a great deal of thought, I was suddenly putting myself forward for speaking engagements on the Life Insurance Association ‘circuit’ in the United Kingdom which then led to a Million Dollar Round Table invitation to speak at the Main Platform in San Francisco the same year. I was spending time working on the business; creating strategies to ensure the continued growth and success of my business.

The Bank Manager had, historically, been someone I approached only for financial support – but he actually became a good friend, as a result of the various lunches I was invited to attend.

Of course, there were some material goals which I turned into Mindchangers:

> My 10% account has made me realise that making money and keeping it is merely a discipline I have mastered.

> My financial portfolio is truly amazing.

> I get such a buzz from the long drive up our tree-lined drive. I can't see myself moving from this place.

> Only a few years ago I was wondering if I would ever get the chance to go skiing again. Now I reward myself with a family trip each Christmas.

> The Chateau in Tuscany is all I ever dreamed it would be. Now I am looking for something with a swimming pool.

When I first put these Mindchangers together I was not particularly disciplined and merely thought of some of my more material goals as long-term dreams. But I found myself setting up my 10% account and I was not only looking for but designing both my ideal home and a rural retreat somewhere abroad.

I now know that had I simply listed all of these goals on a piece of paper I would have sent a message to my sub-conscious that sounded like “Here is a list of things I hope to achieve in the future”; whereas Mindchangers are sending a constant, daily, message to my brain that makes be feel that any goal I set is something achievable: I’m going to make it happen!

Modesty does not allow me to share the results of my own Mindchangers but, suffice to say, I have been extraordinarily pleased with some of the outcomes!

6:4:1

How many of us struggle to tackle a problem or goal because it just seems beyond our capabilities? Maybe we want to lose weight but don’t know where to get started. Possibly we want to spend quality time with our family but never seem to have a spare moment to ourselves. Or perhaps we focus our attentions on a new house but can’t seem to find the discipline to save.

The best way of tackling goals like these is to break things down into smaller parts and handle each component part in order. Great theory, of course, but how does it work in practice? The 6:4:1 is a simple idea which can be committed to a single sheet of paper and can, like Mindchangers, be carried around in a diary. The ‘6’ (although this could be any number) represents key areas of life or business. For example ,the ‘6’ categories might be social, financial, business, health, family and leisure: six categories that broadly cover every aspect of one’s life. The ‘4’ represent the four main sub-headings – ‘keys’, or strategies, if you like – in order that one might work towards a particular objective. The ‘1’ is the very next thing that needs to be done in order to work towards one of these objectives. So, under the category of health one might have ‘lose weight’ as a sub-heading. That is the easy bit. However, the difficulties lie in ensuring that the very next thing we have to do in order to work towards achievement of the goal is as stated: the very next thing that needs to be done. In this example, all too often I have seen people write the words ‘go on a diet’ and, of course, it would seem logical to believe that this is the very next thing that needs to be done. But what about weighing yourself? Starting out ‘with the end in mind’ is certainly an excellent philosophy but one must also identify an absolute start point. A detailed plan can then be put together, as appropriate.

Tackling any goal – or indeed problem – in small, manageable, pieces will maintain enthusiasm and discipline levels. After all, when was the last time you saw a world famous mountaineer attempt to conquer Everest without establishing holding camps at strategic points along the way?

MANAGING YOUR TIME

It is quite obvious that most people appear to have vastly more things to do than they have time to do them. Despite this I'm not hugely keen on time management training but it is vitally important to manage one's time effectively if we are to increase our capacity for more clients and more contacts. Like it or loathe it, effective management of time is a key component of successful business practices.

Of course we have all wanted, from time to time, an extra month a year into which everything could be packed. But this 13 month year can, actually, be achieved, in effect, by working smarter in order to save at least _ hours per day of your precious time. These collective hours could equate to an extra 20 working days or so over the course of the year – hence the 13 month year. So what's the problem when there is huge potential to substantially grow our business?

The real issue I have with time management is that most of us don't actually believe we can manage it effectively – nor can we change it, reverse it or stop it. No technique will achieve this but what we can do, however, is make better use of time. Managing time is about having the skills, knowledge and the correct *state of mind.* I accept that there are techniques that help people to manage their time – the much talked about 'to do' list or time planner can be very useful. But the skill is not just having reminders on our desks but is actually using them and doing so effectively. This, like many things, will depend so much on attitude – our recognition that this is effective – and then applying a discipline to follow it through.

Even more important is that we have to recognise that it is *our* choice whether we 'go with the flow' (often the easy option) or actually address the key issues. There is no such thing as 'I didn't have enough time.' Everyone has the same 24 hours in every day, as far as I know. In simple terms: if a task didn't get done, it is because someone consciously decided not to do it (rightly or wrongly) so it is really an issue of deciding on priorities and making decisions.

For those who would like to start thinking more about how to better manage time, the score sheet below will help you identify what may be some of the main problem areas. It was, and continues to be, a great track to run on for me personally:

Rank 4 (strongly agree) 1 (strongly disagree) Be extreme – try to avoid using the middle ground if possible.					
		4	3	2	1
1.	I know exactly what my objectives are and those of my business.				
2	I can list the most important tasks I do.				
3	When I start a new day, I always know what I need to do.				
4	I usually do the important things rather than tasks that need to be done urgently.				
5.	I usually think about how I organise my time.				
6.	I always complete what I would like to do during a working day.				
7.	I never spend longer on the phone than I should.				
8.	Most of the meetings I attend are a good use of time.				
9.	I usually set realistic deadlines.				
10.	It isn't feasible to reduce the number of visitors I see/time I spend with them.				
11.	I'm good at saying 'no' and avoid getting involved in everything.				
12.	I believe that it is possible to manage my time better.				
13.	I give a reasonable amount of thought to how I do my job.				
14.	The telephone saves me more time than it wastes.				
15.	Rarely do I tend to bite off more than I can chew.				
16.	When I do something, I don't spend too much time on the detail or 'finishing it off'.				
17.	I always make sure that when I'm running meetings, they only last for as long as they need to.				
18.	I tend to focus my time on the things that matter.				
19.	I am good at making my own decisions.				
20.	In my business, people usually complete their daily workload by 5.00pm.				
	Total Score		Totals		
Scoring: 0-39: Oh dear. 40-59; OK but room for improvement. 60-80; Pretty good, but don't get complacent.					

Whilst this time management score sheet will hopefully help identify some key issues, it does not provide answers. The key to managing time effectively does, however, require us to embrace the belief that we are not helpless victims of the commercial world. Instead, we are all responsible for how we use our own time; it is just a matter of how we exercise our choice.

DAILY PLANNING ROUTINE

Most important is that when planning our day we must be free from distractions and interruptions so here are some ideas that I hope will help.

12 Questions to assist in preparing your daily action list:

1. Of my long range high priority goals which should I work on today?
2. What will help me reach these long range high priority goals today?
3. Which projects will give me the highest return on my investment?
4. Is there a deadline to work to?
5. Which project will be the greatest threat to my survival if I don't do it?
6. Which project will be the greatest threat to my company if I don't do it?
7. What project does my superior want me to do?
8. What wasn't completed yesterday that needs to be done today?
9. What do my personal values suggest I should be doing?
10. What does company policy suggest I should be doing?
11. Is there anything else that may yield long term results?
12. What will happen if I don't do it?

8 Questions to help prioritise the daily action list.

1. What will give the greatest long term results?
2. Which item will give the highest payoff?
3. On a long term basis which items will make me feel best to accomplish?
4. Will it help reach my potential?
5. Does it require other people to assist me?

6. Is it a directive from someone who I can't ignore?
7. Which projects does my superior consider most vital?
8. What will happen if I don't do it?

Suggested symbols to use when prioritizing:

A	=	Vital
B	=	Important
C	=	Limited value
X	=	Waste of Time
✔	=	Fully completed
/	=	Partially completed
*	=	Urgent – call for immediate action
()	=	See or refer to
Ⓟ	=	Delegated – initial indicates delegatee (eg "P" is for Peter)
→	=	Carried forward.
←	=	Dropped

HOW MUCH IS YOUR TIME WORTH?

The following table calculates the actual hourly cost of time for people at various income levels. The value of each of your hours – even each of your minutes…is something to bear in mind when you review your diary record. Look at your time as money to invest. At your day-end summary, congratulate yourself for good "investments" – and also pin-point any that may not bear as high a yield.

You are also "investing" the time of persons who report to you, and other people whose time you consume. Consider those costs, too.

Salary Year	**Salary Week**	**Benefits = 40% total salary**	**Total Week**	**Value per hour**	**Value per minute**
5,000	**96**	**38**	**135**	**3**	**0.06**
6,000	115	46	162	4	0.07
7,000	**135**	**54**	**188**	**5**	**0.08**
8,000	154	62	215	5	0.09
9,000	**173**	**69**	**242**	**6**	**0.10**
10,000	192	77	269	7	0.11
15,000	**288**	**115**	**404**	**10**	**0.17**
20,000	385	154	538	13	0.22
25,000	**481**	**192**	**673**	**17**	**0.28**
30,000	577	231	808	20	0.34
35,000	**673**	**269**	**942**	**24**	**0.39**
40,000	769	308	1077	27	0.45
45,000	**865**	**346**	**1212**	**30**	**0.50**
50,000	962	385	1346	34	0.56
55,000	**1058**	**423**	**1481**	**37**	**0.62**
60,000	1154	462	1615	40	0.67
65,000	**1250**	55	**1750**	**44**	**0.73**
70,000	1346	538	1885	47	0.79
75,000	**1442**	**577**	**2019**	**50**	**0.84**
80,000	1538	615	2154	54	0.90
85,000	**1635**	**654**	**2288**	**57**	**0.95**
90,000	1731	692	2423	61	1.01
95,000	**1827**	**731**	**2558**	**64**	**1.07**
100,000	1923	769	2692	67	1.12
125,000	**2404**	**962**	**3365**	**84**	**1.40**
150,000	2885	1154	4038	101	1.68
175,000	**3365**	**1346**	**4712**	**118**	**1.96**
200,000	3846	1538	5385	135	2.24

TIME MANAGEMENT

Listed below are 30 ways to become a more efficient user of time and prepare yourself for astounding success:

Preparation and Organisation

1. Tidy desk.
2. Be conscious of time.
3. Daily List.
4. Delegate.
5. Say 'no' to jobs that aren't yours.
6. Be assertive.
7. Set realistic deadlines.
8. Give yourself private time.

Dealing with Interruptions:

9 Work out who needs access to you at all times.

10 Get your secretary to deal with the rest.

11 Ask the person why they've come to see you.

12 Stand up when they come in.

13 Be ruthless with time and gracious with people.

14 Suggest you fix the meeting later.

15 Make the meeting in the other person's office.

16 Perch on the edge of the desk.

17 Save small talk for the pub or bar.

Meetings:

18. Be conscious of wasting other people's time.
19. Plan the meeting and have a clear objective. Start and end on time.
20. Don't allow meetings to be interrupted.

Dealing with the telephone:

21. Get your secretary (or someone) to field your calls and have a call back system.
22. Make your calls in blocks.
23. Write down the points to raise in the call.
24. Be especially aware of time passing on the 'phone.

Office Systems:

25. Finish one job before you go onto the next.
26. Spend 5 minutes in the morning planning the day with your secretary.
27. Get your secretary to screen mail.
28. Handle each piece of paper only once.

And Finally:

29. Make use of committed time.
30. Put up a clock where everyone can see it.

Potential Time Stealers:

It is all very well being aware of what makes time management effective but we also need to know what obstacles can get in the way so we can avoid or eliminate distractions.

Lengthy discussions on phone or otherwise.
Drop-in visitors / Telephone Calls and other interruptions.
My door is always open.
Drop-in visitors who won't go.
Excessive socializing.
Repeating yourself in personal or 'phone conversations.
Other people rambling on in conversation/discussions or introducing irrelevancies.
Your rambling as above.
Subordinates making mistakes.

Being asked to make decisions below your level of authority.

You losing control.

Doing too much reading.

Data addiction.

Irrational decision making techniques.

Indecision by you.

Making decisions but not implementing.

Fear of small mistakes.

Postponing the unpleasant or difficult.

Doing other people's jobs for them.

Doing too much at the same time.

Doing too much.

Can't get jobs finished.

Other people failing to tell you things you need to know.

Recurrent crisis.

Travelling.

Phoning the same place or person several times when you could have done it in one or two calls.

Spending a long time looking for paper or information.

Paper shuffling in general.

Doing valueless or pointless tasks.

Forgetting to do/say things.

Doing tasks in an illogical or inefficient order.

Not having the necessary information available.

Lack of concentration or your mind wandering too much.

Re-working tasks done inadequately first time round.

Perfectionism in tasks where adequacy would do.

Always looking for mistakes.

Just being aware of these (even if it takes a while to create a great time management system) will help to build an efficient and smooth running business engine.

Buy The Ticket.

A regularly used phrase but one that is applicable to all successful businesses. Consider the nine dots on the page, below, and then re-create these on a separate sheet of paper. Now try connecting all nine dots with four straight lines – and without taking your pen off the page.

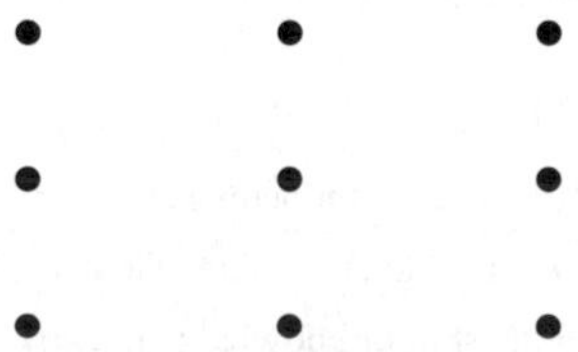

Did you manage it? If you have discovered the answer – or if you have seen this before – you will know that the only way this 'puzzle' can be done is by 'thinking outside the box'. By the way, the actual answer is shown in the End Of Chapter Exercises.

We all have an imaginary 'box' which is, broadly speaking, the lives we live and the businesses we run. For some reason, we believe that the imaginary box represents the boundaries of our thinking and therefore our ability to achieve success.

There really are no limitations: realising we are the ones holding ourselves back can completely change our lives. I hope some of the ideas I have already shared help you break free from the confines of your own imaginary box?

Staying focused is an extremely important part of the process and one way to progress – rapidly – is to 'buy the ticket'. For example, how many times do we find ourselves promising ourselves a holiday with the family or a regular trip to the gymnasium to keep fit? How many times do we start (and end) the diet or promise ourselves that we will pursue a life long ambition; yet discover nothing materialises? Committing to next year's vacation by going out and buying the flight tickets; by joining a gymnasium and booking one-to-one lessons with an instructor; by committing to changing eating habits or by finding the time to structure a detailed plan (how we are going to achieve our future objectives) is the only way we can realistically expect to succeed.

Image Diary. Taking the Mindchanger theme one stage further: the image diary is a collection of photographs of all the things one desires in life – or business. It might be a new motor car or that dream house in the Country. So, purchase a scrap book and collect visual images of everything you wish to achieve. You will be amazed how powerful the 'Mindchanger' is when there is a constant drip feed of visual stimuli as a compliment to a written plan, for example.

Do/Delegate/Ditch. A really simple discipline but one that all successful people apply to their businesses. Whenever we are confronted with a task we need to determine whether it is something only we can do – possibly because only we have the skill or knowledge to carry out the task – or if it is profitable for us to take on the responsibility.

It could well be that the job in hand is necessary but not productive, or it is a job that could quite easily be done by someone else. Prompt delegation is therefore key because procrastination is an enemy to profitable business.

I would go so far as to say that if 'do' or 'delegate' cannot be applied then 'ditching' (eliminating) the task is the only sensible option. We are, of course, sometimes confronted with situations where neither 'do' nor 'delegate' can be applied but where we are reluctant to ditch. For example, a client may advise he 'needs time to think' or wants us to 'follow up again next year'. Well, there is obviously nothing wrong with establishing a follow up system (maybe it could just be something simple like a diary entry) but should we really be factoring the future into today's thinking? If we really can't rid ourselves of something from our desks or diaries at least we should shift it from our minds.

Magic Wand. If you had one wish that would immediately transform your business right now: what would it be? The one thing that would have enormous impact on your business – what would you want? You can have anything at all.

Around the world I have asked that question to literally thousands of people and I have yet to find one person who offered anything other than the most obvious of answers: secretarial support; wealthier clients; a diary full of appointments; more hours in the day; working with clients who only say 'yes'. No doubt all of these things would have a tremendous impact on one's business but what about 'a stack of completed orders ten feet off the ground?' It goes back to what I said before: thinking outside of the box. Whilst I fully accept there is a process we have to go through in order to achieve a particular outcome, very often this does not mean we have to follow a set process. I am not suggesting for a moment we cut corners, but before blindly following, should we not first determine whether the methodology has been created by someone who has, themselves, been successful?

What Can You Guarantee? For many years, sales people from all over the world have approached me in order to help them solve a particular problem. One of the most common is perceived failure on the telephone; making calls. Many believe, wrongly in my opinion, that a successful telephone call is about getting a sales appointment. Whilst I accept this might be the desired outcome it is not necessarily a measure of success or failure. Consider breaking the telephone call down into four component parts and then give yourself a score for each one. Award yourself 30 marks when you pick up the telephone receiver. After all, this is the first part of the process. Award yourself another 30 marks if you dial the telephone number of the person you are trying to contact. Another 30 marks are yours if you make contact with your prospect (and, who knows, possibly even have a conversation?) and then, finally, 10 marks are awarded if you manage to get an appointment.

Suddenly, the individual who has historically 'struggled' on the telephone finds a renewed enthusiasm because at least 90 out of a possible 100 marks are being scored just for reaching the person at the other end of the telephone line. Of course, we cannot guarantee that they will give us an appointment – indeed, I have yet to find someone who has a 100% success rate – but there are parts of the process we can absolutely guarantee and so this must be the focus of our attention.

Triple A Rating. Spend any amount of time studying the key ingredients to a successful business and three elements stand out above all others. These are:

- Activity
- Attitude
- Action

Consider this for a moment. Show me someone who is busy but lacks enthusiasm and commitment and I'll show you someone who is struggling. Show me someone who is extremely motivated but lacks direction (and is therefore not doing as much as he or she should) and I will show you someone who is a pretender to success. Committed, disciplined, enthusiastic and motivated individuals with a strong work ethic epitomise successful people – but only on the face of it. It is those people who apply themselves that are destined to achieve far more than the average individual. If high levels of activity and the right attitude accompany a positive and pragmatic approach then the strongest possible foundations for success have been laid.

We know that if you want to get somewhere you need clarity of vision. You need to have an emotional buzz and deep-routed drive to really want to do something.

Once you have clarity of vision you need commitment. Even if something seems unrealistic the only way to commit is by giving 100%; by not holding anything back. For those that give 100% commitment, everything changes and impossible dreams become possible.

In order to be successful we all need to prepare a consistent strategy for success. Instead of just showing up and trying to be good, we need to commit to being better at what we do: by researching, learning, practising and preparing. We also have to have belief in our ability and know, absolutely, that we will reach the top.

Probably the most important element of all is 'fun' because unless we can enjoy the journey we stand little chance of reaching our destination.

Quotes

“Have the courage to tell people what you do, but never tell them how much you know. Learn to listen and find out how much they know.”

“Learn as much as you can about the products you represent, but always remember that a sale is 75% the art of listening and salesmanship and only 25% product knowledge.”

“Never be afraid to tell someone you don’t know the answer to his or her question. They will appreciate openness much more than listening to you trying to bluff through a situation.”

“Have the courage to fail – that’s how you gain experience.”

“Never, ever, give up. Remember that your next meeting could open up a world of possibilities. ”

“Make friends with wise people.”

“Know your weaknesses. What you don’t do well, have done by people who have strengths in those areas. Your biggest strength is knowing what you can do; not what you can’t.”

TAKING ACTION

1. Score time management strengths and weaknesses regularly. Eliminate time stealers now.

2. Calculate how much your time is worth; if you don't already know.

3. Use at least five of the time management ideas within your life/business.

4. Start an Image Diary.

5. Apply a Triple A rating to everything you do.

Answer to the Nine Dot Puzzle

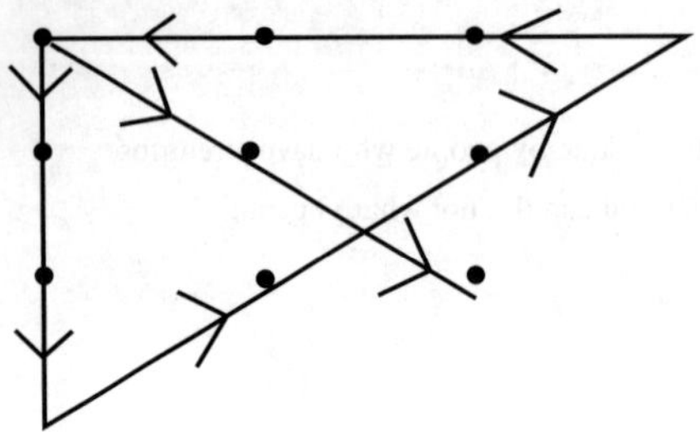

CHAPTER FIVE – EXTRAORDINARY SERVICE

Delivering great customer service on a consistent basis is important to the success of any sales professional.

To create and deliver value for our clients, we have to understand the big picture, while realising that it's the little things that make a difference. We have to easily adapt to change and work quickly in a fast-paced market place where time is money. What follows are a few sales, management and customer service ideas that may help you increase your profitability and productivity, and raise your business to the next level.

Take Time to Think

Take time to think strategically about yourself and your business. Ask yourself difficult questions on a regular basis. What were your top 20 relationships last year and what have you done to keep these clients loyal? Write down the goals you have for yourself and your clients and find creative ways to reach these goals.

When was the last time you audio or videotaped your complete sales presentation and critiqued your performance? Yet consider: what do the great sports teams do every Sunday during the season? They work. What do they do Monday through Saturday? They review, critique and practice.

When do we take time to practice?

Err On The Side Of Activity

What generates the most profit for us? For me, it's face to face time with hand-picked clients. Activity allows each of us to capitalise on the only constant in life – change. The way we service our clients gives us an opportunity to help them through change in their lives; things like health, wealth, taxes, family matters and business issues.

When was the last time we confronted our top 20 clients with a complete review analysis? Properly asked and phrased questions to challenge their thinking and allow them to dream.

By challenging what they do, we help clients stay on track with their dreams. We take them through a thought process to learn about themselves, their children and the organisations in which they are involved. We ask them, "What is it about each of these areas that is important to you?" It is our job to ask the question because we cannot assume the answer. Practice the art of making a point, or what I call, a polite interruption. "Have you considered this? How do you think that could benefit you and your family?

Communication Skills

What is your best communication skill? How do you best use the communication skills you have and how do you develop new and better skills? Our job is to simplify and clarify our client's goals and objectives. That's it. But first, we have to get their information on the table.

Our use of silence in our interviews is one of the most powerful and positive sales tools we possess, providing our prospects and clients with time to think. We must work daily on becoming proactive listeners, because we don't learn a lot when we're talking.

Secondly, never use the words, "Do you understand?" in interviews. Instead, use the four magic words, "Am I being clear?" This way, if the client does not understand, it puts the blame on us, not the client.

Preparation

Always start client meetings with the end in mind. Before each interview, have a specific agenda for clients that orchestrates where you want to be with them when the interview ends. After all, how can we get results if even our clients don't know where we are going?

It is also important to show that we understand the importance of our clients' time and money. We must tell our prospects that in less time than it takes to plan a family vacation, we will take them through our fact-finding process to find out what they really want and need.

Get Quality Personal Recommendations

Would you like to get your clients' best and most responsive personal recommendations? Ask your clients who they rely on for key decisions in their business and personal lives. If they have questions today they could not answer and needed help solving (whether a personal issue, financial concern or business problem) who would be the first person they would call? If this person's insight means so much to your client, it's a good idea to meet him or her. I tell them, "Without your help in getting to these people; even with you as a reference, it would be difficult for me to reach them and get together. What I prefer to do is to have you call them and find a good time we all can get together". This approach works very well with our key centres of influence.

Think about the best clients you have. Someone you have spent hours and hours with over three or four appointments to get to know them better. These individuals with whom you have spent so much quality time and developed such great relationships are the reasons for your success today as well as in the future.

I believe in providing a level of service that keeps people talking; because word of mouth is still the finest and cheapest form of advertising in the world. Service means a guarantee to your top clients in terms of the level of service they can expect – a level of service so high your newest client couldn't do anything than want to recommend you to a friend or work colleague. Providing fantastic service will give your client an instant perspective of the trusted and professional business you run and will, as a consequence, introduce you to multiple networking opportunities. I have never really quite understood why so many people spend so much money advertising their services when, in any market in the world, it takes around seven times as much money to attract one new client as it takes to retain a current client. But to give yourself the best chance of interacting with a client you need to concentrate on a strong communication message; otherwise competitors may target your current clients as their future prospects. So consider minimum standards for client contact, which might look like this:

- For corporate and high net-worth individual clients – four face-to-face contacts every year, including one annual review, one client appreciation event and one seminar or educational function.

- For all other clients – two telephone contacts per year and one annual review (or written offer of annual review) possibly on their birthday or at the policy anniversary. Why not also think about one purely social call?

- A minimum of four paper contacts per year, including two newsletters and two informative or value added mailings.

Of course if you have the ability to send communications by email then a 'thought for the month' (a simple idea or bit of legislative news) might be seen by your clients as something of value.

Of course anyone looking to provide great service needs to have skilled and highly enthusiastic people supporting the practice. Without adequate attention to training it is impossible to expect colleagues to adopt the same work ethic – and continuity is a vital part of good service. Whenever I am looking for a new member of the team I look for attitude and personality because they are so much harder to teach than skill. I need to work with people who share my vision so that I can be confident in empowering them with certain tasks. Total confidence in the team – particularly if they are to be in direct contact with clients – is so important.

If, like me, you already have a fairly large number of clients may I suggest that you divide them into categories? Those clients who you consider to be your best and those who are not quite in the premier league but have good potential need to be separated from those whom you feel you would obtain no further business. Whether you refer to the categories as gold, silver and bronze, A, B and C or 1, 2 and 3, the fact remains that different types of clients will effectively need different levels of service.

Some of the ways we can deliver varying service levels are through differential pricing and target marketing. Differential pricing works on a similar basis to the loyalty schemes adopted by some of the worlds biggest companies. Air Miles is a good example of a successful loyalty scheme and differential pricing works on a similar basis. Our most profitable clients are given the most favourable deals; less profitable clients are charged in a way that encourages them to transact more business so they, too, can enjoy the top service levels and discounts – or they will deselect themselves by looking elsewhere.

Is a client who deselects themselves from your business really such a bad thing? Too many people with potentially great businesses destroy them by clinging to the notion that more clients means more business; a belief is made more difficult to understand because, according to research, just 25% of customers actually generate profit for a business.

Target marketing is a variation of the direct marketing theme whereby low value clients are identified. Mailing them with a fee-based planning proposition allows them the choice to remain with business or de-select in favour of another adviser. But imposing a minimum business or income threshold means, at least, we can be sure that each client is worth at least a certain value to our businesses and therefore means we have sufficient resources to provide a pre-determined service.

For your top clients a simple database or spreadsheet will identify the products or services they have not, hitherto, accessed – so specific targeting to offer discount pricing or certain products that may be of interest is worth considering.

This type of approach will also help with the transition from salesman to professional; if this is, indeed, the perception your clients have of you and your business. What is very important, however, is to determine how to market your practice and what relationship building techniques to use. A very good indication of how a business is perceived by existing clients is the number of unsolicited personal recommendations. If there are not that many clients referring to you on a regular basis then consider some other way that you could lift the perceived value of your business in the eyes of those individuals. Public and targeted client seminars can be a very effective way to generate large volumes of business and, at the same time, raise profile. Client appreciation events (maybe a golf tournament or a cheese and wine evening) are a great way to say 'thank you' and to network.

But there are some even simpler ideas we can incorporate within the business that need not involve any financial outlay. Walking clients to the elevator or door of your office; sending the occasional handwritten note or telephoning, occasionally, just to say 'Hello'. Simple ideas indeed but these are a manifestation of a personal touch that so few businesses possess. Taking great service one stage further: why not send out an annual review check list – an overview of their various policies and overall net wealth? How about helping some of your business clients promote what they do via your website or through client newsletters? Probably the most effective of all: why not add a list of all the services you provide as an appendix to any written communication you send to a client? Unless you have an incredibly successful marketing strategy the chances are your client will only remember you for the last thing you sold; so communicating in this way not only cuts down on the cost of postage but ensures you will be the first person they think of when they need another service.

Here are some other ideas you might like to incorporate in your business:

The First Promise. If you have ever found yourself promising a client, at that very first meeting, that you will be back year after year, without fail, to provide a fantastic service without any intention of doing so then I suggest you need to radically re-think your presentation. How can we expect to be trusted, professional advisers when we are prepared to break the very first promise we make? It is therefore important to know exactly what we can and can't do and then 'promise long, deliver early'.

Similarly if we are of a mind to send out birthday or other greeting cards we need to make absolutely sure we have the resources to deliver: there is little point in sending a birthday card one year and not the next because it creates a complete 'false economy' in the mind of a client. The same is true of regular reviews: only promise what you absolutely can deliver – year in, year out.

Customer Happy Calls. Whether you do this yourself or employ someone to do it for you makes little difference – but have you ever stopped to think about the positive impact a call to each client, post-sale, could have on your business? The call needn't be more than a genuine 'thank you' for their business and to ask for some feedback. What did they think of the service; are there ways we could improve; what would they like to see done differently in the future? The very best source of information for growing our businesses is available from the very clients we represent. Nearly all clients appreciate being thanked and asked for feedback but, just as importantly, we get to deal with any particular problems before they occur.

File Audit. I never cease to be amazed by the number of business people I come into contact with who have very large numbers of clients yet seem to constantly struggle for business opportunity.

It is, of course, easy to occasionally fall into a 'comfort zone' because sometimes too much potential opportunity leads to apathy. So, as both a challenging and exciting solution, I offer the suggestion that next time you have some time to spare – the time that is usually filled with cups of coffee and meaningless conversations in the office – 'review' as many files as is possible. It is always a good idea to run through the files in alphabetical order and to leave a mark for the next visit to the filing cabinets. Taking 20 client files and reviewing each in detail should take no more than about half an hour but the number of business opportunities that will be identified as a result of the File Audit, in a short space of time, is quite astounding.

When running any sort of business it is inevitable we are occasionally going to miss file notes or information detailed in our diaries so a regular review of all client files, in a systematic order, will reveal numerous selling opportunities. Similarly, a regular (once a month?) review of the diary will remind us to follow up on calls and appointments we were supposed to make – but forgot. It's a small investment of time but it produces big results.

In my opinion, excellent service is the key to unlocking massive hidden business potential. Provide stunning service and clients will do a fantastic marketing job for you: they will talk about their 'refreshingly different' experience to others. It will rub off on your colleagues too because consistent customer service is all about ownership and personal motivation. It is something you will come to feel proud of and will reward you and your business handsomely.

Quotes

"Anything will work if you do."

"Work hard and stay in the game - even if it feels like you are not succeeding. Perseverance and hard work ensure success."

"Learn to think big and find ways to associate with the people who are top in your industry – the people who are doing the things you want to do."

"Choose a goal that is way out there – beyond anything you've ever done before. Consider carefully if you want to achieve it. Then, mentally, buy the ticket and go to work. You'll be amazed at how things come together."

"Success is simply a matter of luck. Ask any failure."

"Failures are divided into classes – those who thought and never did, and those who did and never thought."

"Don't compromise yourself. You are all you've got."

TAKING ACTION

1. Create a minimum service standard in your business. Stick to it like glue.

2. Visit your top 20 clients. Ask them for help in building your business through quality personal introductions. Help them to network in return.

3. Categorise all your clients. Know exactly which are profitable and which are not: and invest your time accordingly.

4. If you can, create a database so you know exactly which products and services your clients access. Target future communications accordingly.

5. Organise a client appreciation event. Share the cost with others if you have to but let your clients know you care.

6. Start now – never make a promise you know you can't keep.

7. Commit to a File Audit regularly.

CHAPTER SIX – NETWORK TO THE TOP (THE FEEDING LANE)

Learning to 'think big' and finding ways to associate with the people who are at the top – the people who are already doing the things you aspire to do – is bound to help the growth and development of a successful business practice. But effective networking is more than just finding a mentor who can lend a helping hand from time to time. It is about building strategic relationships that aid the creation of a 'marketing engine'.

Successful business people (who work 'on' their businesses rather than 'in' their business and who run their businesses rather than have their businesses run them) develop value added relationships which ensure a constant source of new business introduction – and therefore revenue. Developing a good network of introducers achieves two things: firstly we can add significant value to the services we are already providing our clients (legal, accountancy, general insurance, stockbroking, banking and so on) but also gain from a hugely efficient and regular source of business introduction. Well established relationships like this ensure unnecessary time and money is spent on marketing and that more resources are made available to provide a first class service. For the small business owner it also takes away a lot of the pressure associated with taking time off from a business; because even when they are away from their businesses their strategic partners are sourcing new client introductions.

It is probably also worth clarifying at this point what I mean by 'the feeding lane'. This is best explained by highlighting the behaviour of salmon; fish that swim up-stream in order to feed. Of more significance, however, is the fact that salmon will only attempt to eat what appears directly in front of them; for no other reason other than their vision is extremely limited. But what this has created, almost by accident, is an extraordinary level of tunnel vision and focus.

So why can't we be the same? Focusing on the things that make us as productive as possible whilst not wasting huge amounts of energy in order to deliver a positive outcome? Most of the very successful business owners I know have built their businesses by either establishing a reputation as an expert in a particular field (and receiving numerous introductions as a result) or else creating lasting relationships with existing clients or other professionals. Subsequently they became known as a trusted and well respected general financial and business adviser.

There is certainly no shortage of opportunity: in the UK alone there are currently 15,000 professional firms (legal and accountancy, mainly) offering financial advice 'in-house' but,, with the ever changing face of regulation, this is expected to drop to a mere 2,000. Clearly these firms do not want to be in a situation where they have to say to clients "Sorry, but we can't deal with you any longer" so this, in turn, represents a fantastic opportunity for us to broaden our horizons and develop new business relationships. Solicitors (lawyers) and accountants (CPAs) have a duty of care to their clients which is why they should be looking to approach other businesses which could assist with the all-round service they have provided in the past. The key to that relationship is reciprocating with such high, quality, levels of service the introducer – who always remains accountable for the referral – trusts his business 'partner' implicitly.

The task is made much easier if we establish a niche. This doesn't necessarily involve specialism but something simple like a particular Unique Selling Proposition. Once it has been established that your business is unique there is a much better chance you will be sought after by both existing clients and professional centres of influence.

There are several examples of this type of business positioning:

- Lowest price/lowest quality.
- Highest price/best quality.
- Best service.
- Friendliest service.
- Widest choice.
- Most convenient.

Competing on price is going to lead to problems because there will always be someone willing or able to offer cheaper products and services. There will always be a competitor with lower overheads, better technology – or it might be prepared to sell at a loss in order to gain market share.

Some clients are willing to have only the best – and are therefore willing to pay for the best. This is why prestige vehicle manufactures continue to sell motor cars and why Rolex and Cartier are still in business. By the way, if you buy a gold Rolex it's not because you want to tell the time!

General financial planning can provide a wide degree of choice, although whatever is offered should be relevant to the particular market place. Sometimes too much choice causes confusion so it might be the most convenient service which appeals: for example, those who wish to purchase from the internet. And it costs absolutely nothing to provide a friendly service although care should be taken to ensure that our client's perception of the manner in which we run our businesses matches our own.

There is certainly no suggestion that any of the above constitutes anything less than a sound business model. To succeed, each must have quality under-pinning the business model, because that is what most prospective clients and customers are seeking. Sometimes (rather unfortunately) it is because they have had a bad experience elsewhere.

Building professional relationships is a process based on universal principles that must be learned, believed and applied. If you think about the relationships most valuable to you, you will probably find that they are based on shared values. If you can identify this as being the case then you have a great opportunity to spend some time discussing almost endless possibilities. Healthy professional relationships are based on mutual respect for the knowledge and expertise both parties bring; so taking the time to study, plan and incorporate some sound business principles will certainly not do you any harm. We all need to be aware that the more we give in terms of respect, the more respect we gain. The more we invest in life and business the more we get back.

It is difficult to over-estimate the real benefits of selling, developing and implementing a long-term financial plan when creating a relationship with a client. But the result is compounded when we are able to successfully integrate the use of other specialists; professionals such as a tax adviser or attorney. This is either because we are looking to provide continuity; encourage long-term relationship-building or provide a quality, all-round, service for less. Whilst we may not be able to directly offer all the services a client may ever need we should be able to call on our business 'partners' who can assist in building a 'One Stop Shop' to customer loyalty.

Identifying the Right Strategic Partners.

The best place to start might be to call up professional advisers you have come into contact with in the past. With a personal introduction from a fellow professional – your prospective client's existing and trusted adviser – there should be no real problems in making an appointment.

When I started my own business I set out to ensure that all my clients, almost without exception, would come by personal recommendation; through either existing clients or professional advisers. I recognised that I did not have what it took to contact 'names' from the telephone directory, so as this was not something I wanted to do so I had to think how I would overcome this prospecting obstacle. To give myself the competitive advantage I knew I needed, I developed an Introducer Pack; a simple presentation document which comprised four sections. The first section was a fax enquiry sheet, which demonstrated to the potential introducer that I operated a system designed to ensure follow-ups and accurate record keeping. Most of all, the fax enquiry sheet was designed to demonstrate a process that was slick and professional. Both adviser and introducer would have a copy of the client introduction so there would never be any lack of communication. Compare this to what most CPAs and Attorneys have been used to in the past – a hap-hazard system of introduction which, usually after only a few months, is exposed as an unreliable and unprofessional arrangement.

The second section is simply a selection of all the standard letters I use in the business process: from the introduction (or welcome) letter through examples of the communications we send to confirm the appointment, a typical recommendation letter and other follow-ups we would send out as part of the sales process.

Section three is an example of a weekly (or monthly) up-date which usually details the name of the client with a brief, one paragraph, explanation of where we are, at any particular time, with the introduced client. This section adds a further dimension to the professional standards we are looking to set; demonstrating a willingness to provide feedback, regularly.

Section four provides an example of a commission schedule assuming, of course, we are looking to share commissions or fees with the introducer; the part of the Introducer's Pack which acts as the commercial 'hook' most professional firms will see as attractive.

Getting an appointment is usually the hard part but we can guarantee failure if we don't even bother to make the calls. To help in your search for positive results may I suggest you are looking for two things: a professional firm with a particular expertise required by your clients and a service standard which matches your own. Instead of simply embarking upon a series of telephone calls 'touting' for business (I have no idea of the success rates of those who cold call but I can imagine it is not very high) don't miss the opportunity to stay completely in control of the first meeting, if one is granted. Imagine calling an Account (CPA) in your area explaining that you are looking for someone to whom you can refer a number of your business clients; the ones who regularly ask for quality tax advice? Imagine asking whether they would be interested in a brief, no-obligation, discussion in respect of you introducing your clients to their business practice? Given that it is likely the answer would be 'yes' you have an opportunity to establish, at that first meeting, whether the prospective introducer has any established relationships with other advisers; relationships which might compromise an association with your own business. If there is no relationship or one in which the prospective introducer does not completely trust you then get the opportunity to demonstrate the unique benefits associated with a strategic relationship between the businesses; starting with a brief look at the Introducer Pack. In my own experience, at least, I can draw on the experience of many previous successes but, at that very first meeting, it was simply a question of presenting a unique and genuine approach to the potential business relationship. The rest is easy.

USING APPROACH LETTERS

Sometimes it might be preferable to send an approach letter prior to making a telephone call. If there has to be a written communication there are a few golden rules; starting with the shape of the mailshot letter itself:

As the two examples show there are vast differences in the structure – and therefore success rates – of different approach letters. To begin, I would always recommend starting with a 'hello' rather than the more formal salutation 'Dear' – simply because it is different and more accurately reflects the greeting we use when we meet somebody in the street, for example.

The first line you write is the line that dictates whether the rest of the letter gets read. No paragraph should exceed three lines and it is always best to write everything in words. The letter should be ordinary but compelling. And there should definitely be no humour or cleverness because then it is unlikely you will be taken seriously.

MAKING COMMUNICATION EASIER

I was introduced to Neurolinguistic Programming (NLP) a number of years ago and have used it, in limited form, successfully since that time. Especially in situations where I am trying to build rapport with a new client or a professional business person.

There are many forms of human communication and, as most of us know, people react differently to certain kinds of stimuli. The vast majority of people react more positively to an image or picture. These are the 'visuals' amongst us. The 'auditories' react to the spoken word or a particular sound and the kinesthetics are emotionally-driven; when the stimulus are feelings and gut-reaction.

To use NLP effectively we must first know what stimulus our prospective client (or introducer) will best associate. It is actually quite easy to find out the best way of communicating in this way – and this simply involves asking a question to which they have to think about the answer. Ask them, for example, who their teacher was at the first school they attended – and then watch their eyes. If they are a 'visual', when thinking, they will look up or appear to be searching for a picture of the individual. For these people try using pictures, illustrations or diagrams when you are trying to make a point. For the individual who is 'auditory' they will almost certainly look sideways (as if to their ears) so this type of individual will probably most enjoy conversations and the spoken word. They will buy a car, not because of its looks or performance, but because of the quality of the sound coming from the stereo. The few people who have a predominance towards emotions will better understand or to empathise based on the way they feel about something. It is possible to react positively to more than one stimulus so it is worth trying two or three questions before deciding what words to use.

NLP, particularly when it is used in conjunction with 'mirroring' (matching of the other person's tone, pace, speed or physical habits) helps build very strong rapport, very quickly. There are plenty of books on the subject and some are well worth the investment.

THE MARKETING ENGINE

There is only one way to create a cost effective, constant supply of new business introductions and it comes by relying upon other people to refer prospective clients. There is no better place to start than with other professionals – but existing clients can be amongst the most reliable of advocates. Creating an environment where prospective clients can meet; what some people refer to as 'favourable circumstances' may be done through, amongst other things, client seminars. This needn't necessarily be a 'turn up and sit down' presentation to hand selected clients. It might take the form of a day, for example, where clients are invited to bring a guest or, failing that, sponsor part of the day. A social event with a brief, informal, opening at the start of the day and then, perhaps, a short presentation during dinner so that people start talking enthusiastically about networking. Consequently they will want to know more about the proposition. Events like this can be very cost-effective; especially when compared to the huge amounts of money spent on buying lists of 'names' and then spending hours and hours cold-calling hundreds of people. Find twenty of your best clients or a few strategic business partners and prospecting, in the way you do now, will become a thing of the past.

People who enjoy making presentations are a rare breed. Public speaking – whether it be to a brand new client or to a group of people when conducting a seminar – holds more fear than just about anything else. People panic in these situations because they are simply not prepared. So knowing your subject, how the presentation will fall together and being clear about your audience needs provides most of the confidence required to create something natural, spontaneous and professional. Nervousness and the rush of adrenaline are normal but it is important to positively channel this energy into improving the presentation, rather than holding everything back. Maintain eye contact with your client or prospective introducer and, in the case of a seminar, members of the audience. Use notes, slides or prompts (the Introducers Pack is a good example) because an ill-prepared or poorly structured presentation is likely to undermine your message, however genuine. Involving an audience also generates trust and confidence.

Identifying your strengths in such circumstances also means recognising your weaknesses, however hard to accept. Too many people focus only on their weaknesses rather than their strengths. By all means, try to eliminate the things you find difficult and become more involved in the things you do best.

It is absolutely vital to be in touch with and to know exactly what market and opportunities exist. Do we only want to deal with people earning over a certain figure each year (eg : millionaires) or are we happier at the 'domestic' end of the market? If we are looking to deal with more people, but at a lower profit margin, then we need to adopt, develop and maintain a very streamlined system. If our energies are to be focused within a niche market far more emphasis will have to be placed on quality, rather than quantity. Rather than set standards which are difficult to maintain it is worth giving some thought, at least initially, to the kind of clients and markets with which we are comfortable. Call those your top 20 clients today and set up a meeting with a view to encouraging them to become your business advocates. There is nothing wrong in asking for help. It is an honest and endearing question and anyone who is asked will undoubtedly say 'yes'. Develop quality relationships with selected 'centres of influence' and the steady flow of new introductions will drive your business in perpetuity.

Quotes

"Learn to think big and find ways to associate with the people who are at the top – the people who are doing the things you want to do."

"Life is what happens to you when you are busy making plans."

"Most of my business came because I created networks. Soon you develop a wide reputation as the expert in this or that area but also as a solid, reliable, knowledgeable person."

"Talk to everyone – often."

"Men are convinced by reasons they themselves discover."

"Value must always exceed cost."

"In the middle of difficulty lies opportunity."

"To make progress we must be strong enough to be weak.'

"The results we get in life are based on our approach to life."

"Star performers know the difference between success and significance."

TAKING ACTION

1. Using the following 'marketing engine monthly plan' use the following template to make a 'To Do' list of the opportunities you can create for yourself right now.

MARKETING ENGINE: MONTHLY PLAN

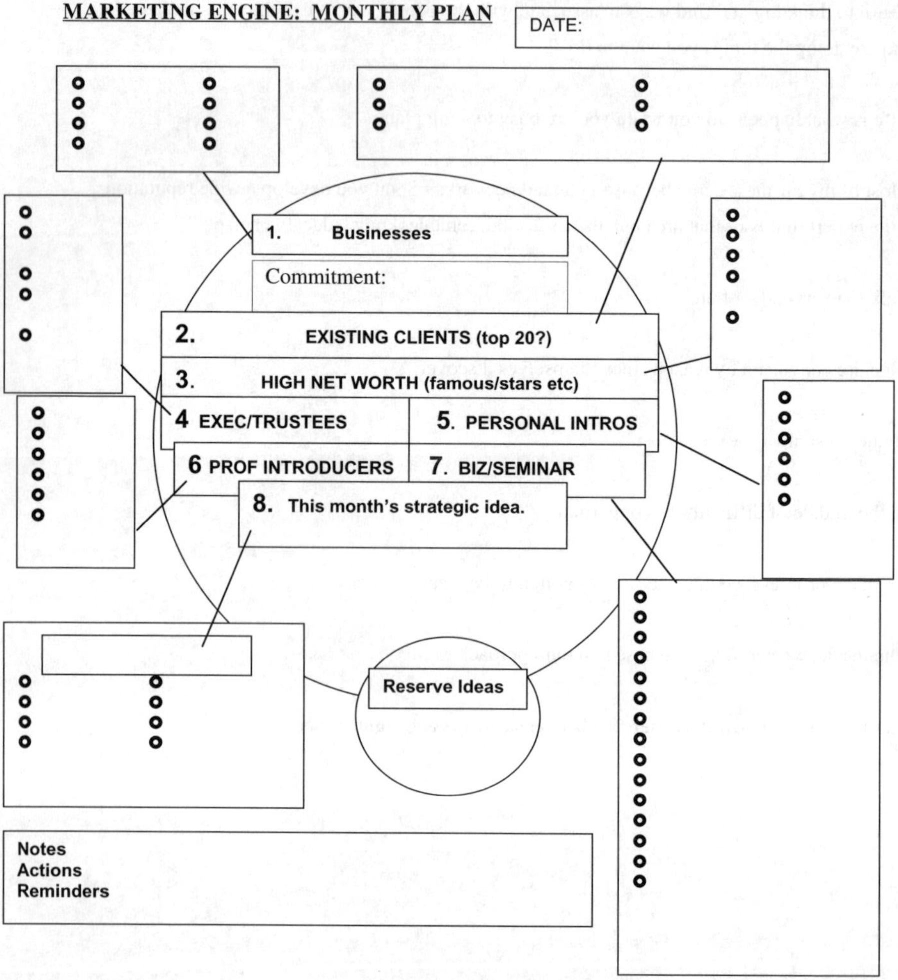

2. In order to make sure sufficient time is put aside to make the necessary calls each day in your diary use the A-E diary system. Each day is divided into three sections: morning, afternoon and evening. Allocate a letter to each of the sections, according to the following suggestions: For guidance purposes A = Sales; B = Background day (preparation); C = Day Off; D = Hotel Day; E = Anything Goes Day. Ensure that in any 30 day period there are at least four 'D' days.

3. Sharpen and develop your skill of conversation. Start a conversation in an elevator, on a seminar or arrange some other form of public speaking.

4. Create a list of six prospective professional introducers and twenty top clients. Call them and ask for a meeting to discuss ways you may help one another.

CHAPTER SEVEN – LESS IS MORE

The inspiration behind this particular chapter was one of my Mindchanger cards; written several years ago. Think about 'Less Is More' for a moment and consider the benefits to a business concentrating on simplicity.

In the insurance profession, in particular, there seems to be a fixation with raising turnover; that the only consistent measure of success seems to be the top line. Why? What business owners should be concentrating on is profit. After all, it's that which really counts. Consider how many other business people you know who said they earned more when they were a small, manageable, business?

It's astonishing to meet so many people who continue to struggle with a business they are not really in control of; doing the things they feel obliged to do rather than the things they truly believe is good for profit. The problem is we don't tend to concentrate on our strengths because it seems difficult to delegate the non-productive jobs – and it is unpalatable to outsource other disciplines, even if they are not really a core activity. But look at any really successful business person and they don't worry about a loss of control. They know if they don't change the way they work, constantly, they'll spend less and less time doing the things that are best for their business: being with clients.

If analysed in detail we would probably find that there are dozens and dozens of tasks that demand our time but very few that have a positive commercial impact. So the question is: do we merely want to survive or do we want to thrive? Attempting to be all things to all people simply does not work. There is, of course, nothing wrong with offering a comprehensive service but it's important to know what we can deliver, effectively and profitably, and those things which need delegating or outsourcing.

To start with it is important to analyse the existing business in detail and to question everything. Decide what works and what doesn't; then eliminate, by one means or another, the things that cost, rather than generate, two of the most valuable of all assets – time and money.

Another reason for the need to take a close look at what we are doing, right now, is because business never stands still. It is a changing world where only the pragmatic, resilient and courageous will survive. However, with careful planning a potential threat becomes a fantastic opportunity. Survive or thrive: it's our choice.

CREATE A STRONG POSITIONING STATEMENT

Remember the last time you were asked by someone what you did for a living? What did you say? Like me, if you've ever found yourself in the terribly difficult position of not wanting to say 'I'm a life insurance salesman' but couldn't think of an alternative, consider the following. Imagine, for the moment, you are in an elevator that stopped at each of three floors, before you get out at the fourth. The first floor sees the owner of a small business get into the elevator. 'What do you do for a living?' he asks. 'I help business owners protect their assets from creditors and I show them how to increase, protect and preserve their wealth' you reply.

At the next floor a lady who is obviously approaching retirement, but also appears to be a person of some financial means, steps into the elevator. 'What do you do for a living?' she asks. I'm a Wealth Preservation specialist'. I specialise in tax mitigation and estate planning so that individuals can get the best for themselves and for their intended beneficiaries'.

At the third floor a lady of about 35 steps into the elevator with you. 'What do you do for a living?' she asks. 'I help my clients, most of whom have children, to reduce or eliminate their debts, plan for future events such as school fees or other future goals and I start to help them design a wealth creation strategy for the future'.

For a variety of reasons we can sometimes feel uncomfortable referring to ourselves by a particular title; maybe because we do not wish to be labelled. In the example above we have been asked the same question three times but on each occasion have given different answers. The truth of the matter is that we are specialists in all these areas but positioning ourselves by responding not just to a clearly identified need but also talking a language to which another person will most easily relate. For example, it is no good talking about life insurance to a retiree (unless it is to deal with estate taxes) anymore than we would talk about wealth management to someone who clearly struggles to survive financially.

We all fear rejection which is why, when confronted with a question like 'What do you do for a living?', we would probably rather say nothing than come out with an inappropriate answer. So why not think about communicating in a way that is far more likely to create a positive response?

Another area in which we tend to have problems is calling on the people we know. In the early days, despite what my manager told me, I was always trying to avoid calling my friends and family because I didn't know how they would react to an approach. But I was never able to explain why I had such a fear of contacting those closest to me. Ironically, it should have been those people I was calling first. But I soon realised that even if I couldn't help these individuals through the service I provided I could still ask for their help in becoming advocates of my business. I realised that anyone who became a client or was prepared to endorse the services I provided to others was a very valuable asset to the business.

When I first joined the financial services profession I was very lucky because I worked with a man who was a fantastic networker and who could powerfully communicate his message in almost any situation. One of the things I always used to remember him saying to the people he knew well – and which was an approach I later adopted with considerable success – was 'I have no reason to expect that you would do business with me simply because we are friends, but I didn't think you would respect me if I didn't ask. Because of the nature of the business that I am in, I'd rather call you three years too soon than one day too late. Do you have any objection in getting together with me on a professional basis?' This man, my manager, taught me that my prospects were all around me and that I shouldn't be guilty of making presumptions about any of them. At times, when I would sit at my desk confronted with the prospect of a 'telephone session' he would ask me 'What's the worst thing that could happen if you make a call?' I would usually answer 'They might say No'. He would see the apprehension in my face but then, calmly, ask 'What's the worst thing that could happen if you don't make the call?' It's then that I would really start to think. It's then I would remember the commitment I was agreeing to make when I first came into such a noble profession.

A very effective way to ensure that we all make that next telephone call is to put a note on, or near, the telephone that states 'If you knew for certain this prospect or client would die or become disabled three months from today, what would be the right action to take now?' Of course, the answer is 'Make the call, ask for the order and, whenever possible, recommend a higher amount of insurance or other products'. Something simple like this keeps us doing the right things, rather than doing what we think we need to do in order to win the approval of others.

The thought of being rejected creates a fear which even the best of us find hard to manage. But acting in spite of the fear is what separates the extraordinarily successful few from the rest.

THE CLIENT LADDER

Several years ago I was speaking to my CPA; a tax adviser who I had worked with for many years. Such was the level of his expertise he received not just a number of introductions from me but would also generate a large percentage of his new clients from advertising and client referrals. Despite the pressures of an ever increasing workload he was doing well.

Over a period of time the quality of service he was providing started to diminish. He was spending more and more time with clients who were clearly not profitable for his business. In turn, he was neglecting his very wealthy clients who ran their own successful businesses. By now he was starting to recognise the problems and so called me in one morning for a coffee. He wanted to know how he might continue to build his 'top line' whilst eliminating the expense of dealing with fairly non profitable clients.

My answer to him was simple: I told him to double his fees.

His response, not untypical of most people who cannot see that 'less is more' was 'But I would lose half my clients!'.

Think about this response. Double his fees; lose half his clients. Where's the problem?

I told him that when I was a manager of a large life assurance company I would come across associates, every day, hoarding hundreds of client files because they somehow felt reassured that by having a large number of clients they could ensure success. Forgive me for pointing out the obvious but our clients will not take the trouble to contact us unless we fulfil the first promise we ever make: to build a long-term relationship built on professional trust. I would argue that we cannot call clients prospects when it has been a number of years since we saw them last. These people are not prospects, they are suspects – and if they have no loyalty towards us they will turn out to be a business liability, not an asset.

It is not about numbers, it is about quality. Fifty clients who fit, absolutely, the type of profile of the individual we want to build a relationship with is infinitely better than a list of one thousand names and addresses. Yet one of the most repeatedly asked questions in our profession is 'How do I obtain more clients?' How about changing the mindset and thinking about 'How do I obtain more quality clients?'

Building a great business is about targeting those people who can really add value to what we already have in place. Write down the names of your top 20 clients or contacts and set a goal to do two things. Firstly that you will endeavour to build a really good relationship with that person; to the point where you can speak with them openly and honestly. If, of course, that point has already been reached, then great. The second point is to arrange a meeting and ask them for their help. Contrary to what many people think ('I simply cannot ask one of my best clients for help – it wouldn't be right') requesting assistance with the building of a business in mind will only achieve something for the business owner if there is also a benefit for the client. As we know, the less time we spend looking for new clients the more time we can dedicate to providing a superb level of service. But how many of our clients are aware of that simple fact? It is our pride that stops us asking for help because we (wrongly) believe it is a sign of weakness. Why should that be? Communicated in the right way, it can be flattering for a client to know that we would like to meet other people who have similar businesses or net wealth – and the number of personal introductions that can be received by simply identifying our top 20 clients is quite astonishing. Setting a meeting agenda to run through, as a reminder, how we run our businesses; the services we offer; how we aim to identify two or three people our client could introduce us to and then demonstrating the value added services we can offer as a result of spending less time marketing our businesses.

Once you have your introduction system off to a fine art you might then like to create a client 'ladder'. This simply involves creating parameters within your business, such as the number of clients you will have at any one time. Then the goal is to find new clients who are good enough to sit within the boundaries you have set. For example, let's say we decide to work with a maximum of 100 clients and a personal introduction is effected from a good client. If the referred individual, or business, does not offer the same business opportunity as an existing 'Top 100' client then you would simply not be able to take them on; instead referring them to another adviser. Conversely, if a new prospective client is introduced and they are someone with whom we wish to build a business relationship then we have to delegate the service of another client (number 100 becomes number 101 on the list) to another adviser: maybe a junior adviser or paraplanner. This system might, on the face of it, seem beyond the scope of many businesses but it is a goal worth aspiring to achieve. You will also find more people aspiring to become one of your 'Top 100' clients – simply because of the exclusivity of what they see as a 'club'. And if clients appreciate the service being provided they will constantly ask what they need to do to remain a client.

Finally (and probably the most important thing) always say 'Thank you' for any help or personal recommendations offered. A genuine appreciation of the way someone might be helping us build our business will ensure the referral cycle continues.

ARE YOU IN BUSINESS OR ARE YOU IN SALES?

The answer has to be 'in business'. It doesn't matter about your current status providing you adopt the mindset of the business person. Once again, the on/in concept needs to be considered. We need to know, absolutely, what are our most valuable assets and what our time is worth. We must seek to improve knowledge and our support systems. We must improve personal and business relationships; increase our contacts and know exactly what we have to do to improve our income. We must live balanced lives and reach for our goals. We must be aware of the opportunities in our market place and we must know our market. We must know when it is time to ask for a helping hand and time to have others share in our success. After all, what is wrong with trying to be the best?

So let's consider, for a moment, what an ideal 'less is more' business might look like. First, we might wish to insist that all our clients have a minimum income of $75,000 per annum (£50,000) or they have a net wealth of at least $1 million (£600,000). Before the meeting we might wish to write to the client in order to confirm the arrangements and to ask them to compare any information which might make our time with them more productive. Should a client ever take the trouble to visit the office then the person who would normally greet visitors should be briefed with the name of the individual and the estimated time of arrival. It goes without saying that we should always appear smart and well organised.

The purpose of the meeting is to build a relationship; to tell the prospective client about the services available and the ways in which they could benefit over the many years ahead. Before gathering all relevant information it is important to know, exactly, the proposition you are trying to communicate.

During this first meeting we are simply asking ourselves 'Does this prospect satisfy my client criteria?', 'Can I work with this individual in the future?' and 'Does this person appear to be a decision taker?' May I suggest we avoid falling into the tempting trap of subconsciously making excuses for a prospective client in order to try to find ways to justify a working relationship? It is our own indiscipline which will have the biggest negative impact so it is important to be selective.

Once it has been decided whether or not we really want this person in our lives, I would suggest we need to look at three things. The primary consideration must be to help clients see, clearly, where they are now, especially in financial terms, before we look at where they want to be at some future date. Of course, the most important thing is to start designing a plan in order to bridge the identified gap.

Whether or not a fee is charged for the first meeting can be discussed at this stage but I always feel it is appropriate to deal comprehensively about the difference between fee-based and commission-based advice before anything else because it avoids any last minute problems.

At the end of the meeting – and if the prospective client seems likely to be suitable for our business – then the appropriate agreements can be signed and the next meeting set. Even if it is unlikely that their individual client will be suitable for our business we should still endeavour to leave a favourable impression so that there is still a willingness to recommend others. Ultimately – and I think this is the same for all of us – we should be trying to send new clients away from every meeting with the prospect of a better future than at the start. It is important they see us as the professionals we should be so when talking about building a relationship with them over, hopefully, a lifetime we need to discuss not just their rights, but ours too. Relationships are not all one way and professional advisers are partners, not employees.

Building a successful business practice is about achieving goals; not just about trying hard. Providing a comprehensive and quality service will generate fantastic results. Communicating our message, regularly, will help us acquire many new clients and people cannot help wanting to become clients if they know what we do, assuming there is a perceived need.

WHAT EXACTLY IS SUCCESS?

Let's imagine you are one of thirty associates in your company and your goal is to be number one. As there can only be one number one will this mean that everyone who does not make it to the pinnacle of the company is a failure? The answer, to my mind, is 'of course not'; success is not a comparison of one person to another, a person's environment or a person's past. If we must compare, success is a comparison of an individual to their own potential. An individual does not have the right to judge another based on their definition of success and, in the same way, we do not have a right to judge others.

But there is another thing that sets successful people aside from the rest: they do many of the things they don't really like doing, but do them anyway, in order to get the things they want. People who fail still want these same things but won't do the things necessary to get them. They are motivated by comfort zones.

Ask yourself how many things you are willing to go without in your life because you don't like to do the things that, if done, would get them for you? Unfortunately, most of us do not like running at the front in life: it is far more comfortable hiding at the back, out of the spotlight.

Success is about the progressive realisation of a worthwhile, pre-determined, personal goal. We are not immediately successful the day we achieve our goal but rather on the day we set the direction and keep moving. I have a note written at the front of my diary that summarises this concept: 'You never fail until you stop trying'. The idea of comparing one person to another in order to determine success is crazy but why do so many people fall into this obvious trap? The reason: it begins early in childhood. How many times did we come home from school, complaining that another child had more toys, a nicer house, a bigger dad, more freedom, more, more, more? Success for children – unfortunately an in-bred trait – is not what the child is or has, but what he is or has in relation to his environment.

There is one very profound and interesting fact surrounding the conscious and sub-conscious mind – and these are important when understanding what drives some people and hinders others. The conscious mind can distinguish between what is real and what is imagined whereas the sub-conscious cannot. The sub-conscious does not know the difference between a real experience and one that has been vividly imagined. It does not know the difference between a real failure and one that is imagined. Likewise it does not know the difference between a real success and an imagined success. The sub-conscious mind also resists a new idea the first time it is exposed to it. For these reasons, you can imagine the potential benefits of using Mindchangers.

We all have one thing in common: we have arrived physiologically and mentally at our current status through a similar route. We may have been brought up by different parents in different parts of the world; we may not be the same sex, religion, colour, age or nationality But believe me, we have one major thing in common – we have both been conditioned by an environment over which we have no control. Our early childhood – prior to age seven – has more to do with our current level of success than any other single factor. It is for this reason that Mindchangers takes on such an important role in taking us from our current position in life to a new level. Most people in sales have a self-imposed ceiling of thinking. The feeling is not a physical barrier but an internal, mental, one. It is almost like an internal target. Indeed, most sales people who have ever worked under a target system would agree that the average person quits when they reach their target.

The objective of this book is not for me to tell you what you have to do to become successful, nor is it to tell you what I did to become successful because success is a personal thing. It is different things to different people. What are you after? What's important to you? To achieve your own level of success you must first recognise that you are different from others. Your wants are different, your needs are different, your problems are different, your life is different. Therefore, your goals must be different.

So, we have arrived at a definition of success: it is the progressive realisation of a worthwhile, pre-determined, personal goal. We never fail until we stop trying. Our own future is up to each one of us. We must stop looking back; instead we must look around and consider where we are emotionally, psychologically and physically. We must take the responsibility for where we are and where we want to go in life. And start today.

I once read an article that was based on a study of millionaires. The study sought to determine the key commonalities between ultra-successful individuals. These were as follows:

- The ability to cut through to the core of the problem and take charge of a situation quickly.
- The habit of positive action.
- Hard working.
- Enthusiasm.
- A definite objective.
- Mentally tasked.
- Physically fit.
- Always involved.
- Give more than they take.
- Learn to motivate.
- Loyal.
- Learn from adversity.
- Strong commitment.
- Persistent.
- A risk-it-all-attitude.
- Confident.

Wouldn't it be fantastic if we could have all of these attributes? The next question: why can't we? That said, if we could only ever adopt one skill then it must surely be that we are effective at prospecting. Effective prospecting is the most important sales technique we will ever need to master. It is more important than good sales presentations or the ability to answer client objections. The best sales people are at their best when they are getting information and building relationships. Why is it we hear so many people say that we need to plan our sales presentations? If we plan a sales presentation, we are making the basic assumption that everyone who buys from us is going to buy for the same reason.

If you have been selling even a short while you will know it isn't completely about planning. The job of professional selling is to discover prospective clients' needs, desires, opinions, problems, prejudices, attitudes – and to help them arrive at a conclusion on some or all of those things. An effective sales presentation is not a presentation but a conversation; a two-way conversation, not a one-way conversation. Similarly, concluding business with a well qualified prospect is a natural end to everything we have done in the sales process that is correct and effective. We can make people buy things they don't need but we can't make people buy things they don't want.

After sales service is the 'glue' that keeps clients loyal; it keeps them continually coming to us for advice and means they are willing to offer us personal introductions. Poor sales people take the money and run; forgetting that it is considerably more time consuming and expensive to acquire a new client than it is to provide a great service to an existing one. This is the key to building trust. People buy from people they trust; not people they like. Therefore the key to building trust is simple: promise a lot – and deliver more. Do what you say you will do and then more. Honour your commitments, communicate with integrity and be a resource for your client; not just a sales person selling a product or service. Successful sales people don't sell price, they sell value. The price will always seem high if the value of the service you provide is perceived as low. If clients bought cheap they would all be using the supermarkets and the internet to buy financial services. Every client, almost without exception, worth the investment of our time is the one who wants best value. If we sell value we will never have to worry about losing business to a competitor based on price.

So what stops us achieving all these goals? Is it because we have a poor attitude? Is it because we use time badly? Or that we lack specific goals? Is it because we do not have any self discipline or because we procrastinate? Is it a lack of concentration; neglecting self evaluation and appraisal; the inability to cope with rejection; the inability to accept failure from time to time; a lack of creative imagination or just a basic lack of desire? Try evaluating yourself in all these important areas and concentrate, for the next 30 days, on improving just one area. Do not accept mediocrity as you attempt to improve your techniques and disciplines but always try to 'go the extra mile'. The courage needed to take that one extra step (or sometimes even being prepared to take one step back in order to take several steps forward) is where we lose a lot of would-be successes in life. Develop the habit of giving more than you get, not less.

Quotes

"Everyone wants to be right but no-one stops to consider if their idea of right is right."

"You can't do something you don't know if you keep on doing what you do know."

"You can level your own playing field by realising life only becomes fair."

"To improve as a golfer – and as a person – you have to rise and fall alone and to learn exactly why it is you have risen or fallen."

"I tell my kids what my mum told me. Everyone has to have a plan and for every plan you have, you need three more to back up the plan. I planned things even as a kid."

"A great pleasure in life is doing what people say you cannot do."

"The difference between a successful person and others is not a lack of strength, not a lack of knowledge, but a lack of will."

TAKING ACTION

1. Decide how many clients you can realistically manage personally. Create a business ladder and decide upon the parameters of that ladder.

2. Write to, or call, all your 'ladder' clients in order to explain what you want from them and what you will provide, in terms of service, in return.

3. Clear all the names and tasks from your diary or work sheet that have been there for more than three months. Names in the diary for more than three months are no longer prospects, but suspects.

4. Make a list of all the things you know you can delegate to someone else – and do it now.

5. Try to cut down your working day by one hour initially and then, eventually, take one day off every week. You'll still find time to get everything done.

6. In less than 25 words, what is your major purpose in life?

7. Evaluate, again, your strengths and weaknesses and commit to improving at least one area over the next 30 days.

8. Consider ways you can add in greater value to your business proposition – and implement the plan now.

CHAPTER EIGHT – GETTING YOUR NAME UP IN LIGHTS

So many of us miss one of the best opportunities of all to promote our businesses in the best way possible; by using the Media to endorse our professional standards. Many of us, however, fear this very effective way of communicating because it is something of an unknown quantity. But build a good relationship with the editor of a local or national newspaper or with the controller of a radio station and prospecting will become infinitely easier.

Why talk to the media ?

Quite simply it's a marvellous opportunity to promote you or your company. A few column inches in a newspaper or a three minute radio interview is a chance for you to get your company name and services noticed. In an age where branding is evermore important this could be crucial for your business. For many years companies have recognised the power of advertising and they spend many thousands of pounds or dollars crafting advertisements when, sometimes, a more powerful argument can be made through media relations. It also raises the profile of the company internally and therefore can be very encouraging for staff.

Why we avoid talking to the media

Fear of saying the wrong thing; fear of being misquoted; fear of being 'shown up'. Fear stems from the unknown; not knowing how a journalist works and thinks or the constant worry that he or she is simply there to put the knife in or catch us out. Contrary to popular myth, and as any study of the media will reveal, the vast majority of interviews are designed to elicit information and not to make a fool of the interviewee. Of course, there will be moments in one's career when there will be tricky interviews to handle but you should be aware that once you embark on a relationship with the media you must expect to be asked to comment in good times and bad.

Preparation

The best spokespeople in the media today are those who prepare carefully before each media appearance. It's true to say all those silver-tongued businessmen and politicians you see and hear have thought very carefully about what they are going to say beforehand. They have also worked out the audience they are addressing because a message which is suitable for local radio may be too basic for, say, the readers of a national newspaper. That, fundamentally, is the secret. If you know what your message is in advance you are more likely to get that message across; even if the journalist fails to ask exactly the questions you want. Bear in mind that a journalist may have some idea of where he or she wants to take the interview but a good journalist is always receptive to interesting information. Therefore, if you have something worthwhile to say make sure you get your point across.

But how can you stand a better chance of grabbing the journalist's attention?

Examples, facts or human interest stories are great because they provide the evidence to any point you may make. Too often a journalist will hear how marvellous, far reaching, focussed or technologically superb the interviewee is, but why should the journalist believe it? He or she needs evidence and evidence can come by way of a fact or story.

It is a good idea to construct a fact sheet setting out the more interesting aspects of your company, its services or any issue which you may be discussing with the media. What makes you special? Perhaps yours is the only business in your area which has staff who can speak five languages? Did you win last year's Business Of The Year award? Are you the fastest growing company in your town or city today? Make a note of any interesting research data and examples, which might make a story more rounded and try to show your organisation in a more positive light. Keep this record up to date and encourage others in your company to contribute to the list. Even a noteworthy conversation with a client can provide useful for the newspaper journalist.

National and local media

The national media has a much clearer agenda and is more difficult to influence than the local media. The local media are an easier and more accessible target, constantly on the look-out for stories with a local flavour, especially those with an element of human interest.

What information and when?

Don't be afraid of taking the bull by the horns and contacting the media. These days the media have many column inches to write and hours of airtime to fill so, more often than not, welcome enthusiastic interviewees. Having said that you need to have something worthwhile to say. You may, for example, have an enticing story about one of your clients: human interest stories are extremely important to the media as not only can they stand up as an interesting piece of journalism in their own right but also they provide the basis on which to talk about a wider issue.

Alternatively, your views and expert knowledge are important to the media at various moments in the financial calendar. Any issue which touches on your business or area of expertise is, in essence, a chance for you to voice your opinions and therefore provide an opportunity for your organisation to gain a higher profile.

In addition, try to think like a journalist. What are the concerns of his or her audience at that particular moment and what is topical? Often journalists need an expert view on these matters to provide balance or weight to what they intend to write or say. Remember the journalist is not an authority on every subject he or she covers so they need your help.

How to contact the media

Press releases are a good way of contacting many journalists at one time. The downside is that all journalists have desks overflowing with literature so unless the story catches their attention straight away, your press release is destined for the waste paper basket. Therefore you need to begin the press release with a good punchy introduction. Make sure the information you give is clear and always give contact telephone numbers because if the journalist is hooked he or she may call you for more details or, in some cases, all they will require is a single quote. Alternatively, if you would like to appear on a specific programme or in a journal it can be profitable to contact the journalist direct with your idea or story. At the end of the day, though, if you wish to have a sustained relationship with the press it helps to get to know one or two individuals and build a good contact.

Reputation

It is always worthwhile getting to know key journalists. Journalists are no different from anyone in business in that they like to deal with people they know and can depend on. It makes sense for anyone writing an article to call one or two individuals who he or she knows will have something interesting to say. This is a far more profitable use of time than ringing an experienced interviewee who may take three times as long to interview. This is why the same individuals are quoted in articles and appear on radio and television programmes time and again: they are tried, trusted and reliable. It also helps to have a reputation as someone who is always available and will not let you down; someone who will return calls at awkward moments and will happily appear live on the 6.00 am breakfast show!

Lunches

Inviting journalists to lunch can be helpful for both parties, although it can be a waste of time unless you prepare carefully. Think through potential issues and possible stories you can discuss. Do some homework on the journalist beforehand: who does he or she write for and have they written any interesting articles recently you can talk about? Read through any press articles which may have been written about your company because this is where the journalist will go to get an impression of the sort of business you run. Listen carefully to what the journalist has to say because he or she may give away clues about how their paper views your business sector.

Newspaper Interviews – Responding to a Press Enquiry

If a journalist calls you out of the blue, it is important to make some initial enquiries as to who they are and find out things like the interview topic. Ideally, you should tell the journalist you need a few moments to consider your response and promise to return their call within a specific time-frame. Bear in mind the journalist may be on a deadline so you need to convince him or her you will respond and will do so promptly.

Language

Journalists are always looking for interesting language and good quotes, if you provide them with several catchy phrases they are very likely to print them. If they are spectacular enough they may even end up in the headline or spearheading a feature. Remember, though, quotes can be used in isolation so try to imagine your sentence when taken out of context and splashed over the front page of a tabloid. Would you be as happy with it then? Avoid too much confusing industry jargon and corporate or marketing speak as they only serve to confuse. It may surprise you to learn that often the journalist "got it wrong" purely because he or she did not understand what the interviewee was talking about!

Time

The fundamental difference between press and broadcast interviews is the time factor because there simply isn't the time for lengthy explanation and analysis. The television News Bulletin will often contain less than 4,000 words – fewer than in a single news page of a national newspaper. Therefore, the length of your interview may vary from 10 minutes for a chatty informational piece on local radio to 3 minutes for a corporate interview and 30 seconds for a sound bite on a news channel.

Bear in mind many interviews will be pre-recorded and edited later; a half hour recorded interview can be broadcast as only a few short clips. It is therefore very important that you repeat your key message several times during the course of the interview to ensure it makes it onto the programme.

Local radio and television are closer to a popular tabloid newspaper than a broadsheet in their depth of coverage. Remember the word is BROADcast. Both are mediums of mass communication. Your audience is the person in the street, and in talking to them you should never over-estimate his or her knowledge or common sense. Remember, too, your radio audience may be listening to you while driving or making breakfast, and that very few people concentrate totally on what is on their TV screen. What you say must be clear, concise and interesting.

Pre-Interview Homework

Before going anywhere near a microphone, do your homework. Find out everything you can about the interview. For example:

- What programme you are appearing on?
- Is it live or recorded?
- What context is your piece being used in?
- Who else is on the programme?

The Interview

Always find out what the first question is just before the interview begins. This allows you a few seconds to think of a good first answer, which should be clear and engaging enough to hook the listener.

You must answer the question but remember you are not on trial. This is a conversation and therefore once you have dealt with the question feel free to move on to the things you want to say.

Try to restrict your answers to around 30 seconds. If your answers are too long it bores the audience. If they are too short you get more questions and thus lose control.

Keep it clear and simple. Let the examples tell the story and provide interest.

Visual Impression

On radio and television it is important to look good as well as to sound energetic and enthusiastic. Don't let your eyes wander from the interviewer. Don't be frightened of using your hands to emphasise points. Smile where appropriate. When dressing for television bear in mind stripes and checks can "shimmer" on screen so stick to reasonably plain colours. Black and white don't work well, especially when worn together. You also need to avoid wearing anything distracting such as a security pass, fob watch or an odd tie.

Tricks of the Trade

Of course you need to exercise reasonable caution when talking to journalists, so:

- Be clear in your mind beforehand what you can talk about and what it would be imprudent to discuss.

- You can feed journalists non-attributable information but tread with care. It takes a bit of experience to know how to handle off the record comments. You can always give journalists background information, which is not sourced to you, but 'quotable' quotes made "off the record" can occasionally backfire.

- Remember a journalist is a journalist 24 hours a day so be sure not to reveal information you may later regret. This is particularly common after a alcohol-induced lunch for example – an extremely fruitful time for journalists to glean gossip!

- Be aware that journalists will occasionally be looking to confirm a rumour and can use cunning tactics to do so; a journalist who claims to know some confidential information may well be doing nothing more than fishing.

Tricky Interview Topics

You always have the right to say 'No' to a journalist and in very difficult circumstances, especially if there are legal implications, this may be the wisest course to take. Some journalists deliberately attempt to wind up their interviewees, so the trick is to refuse to be wound up. However, bear in mind the journalist has a job to do, his audience to inform and an editor to satisfy. Treat a journalist as a professional – you can say "No" firmly but politely – who knows when you may be talking to him sometime in the future?

Many people ask me if it is worth the effort. My reply most definitely. I have benefited from a huge upsurge in business since I became well-known within the media circles; even just at a local level. Clients and potential customers become incredibly more confident and trustworthy when dealing with someone more 'high profile' than a competitor. I appreciate it appears a daunting task; and a tricky step to take but consider the benefits – and try it out!

Quotes

"You can determine what your future income will be and accomplish it."

"You have unlimited opportunities for advancement along paths of your own choosing."

"Habits die hard! What you are or what you do as the result of habit. You have created what you are today. If you are to change what you become you must form new habits. Either you will form new habits beginning today or your life will continue as in the past."

"Be understood. Education is only half the battle. Trying to impress upon people how smart you are won't make you successful. Transferring knowledge into concepts that can be easily understood is the key."

"Network. Create networks and centres of influence. Soon you will develop a reputation for being the expert in a particular field."

"Well done is better than well said."

"Every job is a self-portrait of the person who did it. Autograph your work with excellence."

TAKING ACTION

1. Contact your local Radio station and offer your services, free; in case they are thinking about offering their listeners advice on matters such as tax (towards the end of the tax season) or how to budget for, and spend on, holidays. Other topical issues such as school fees planning or estate taxes might also be useful, depending on the audience.

2. Get a professional to take some quality photographs and compile your own personal introduction; detailing experience, skills and knowledge. Send this personal introduction, together with a photograph to five selected local or national publications and invite them to contact you.

3. Keep a detailed record of the business you generate from each of these opportunities and report back, from time to time.

4. Try to build a close working relationship with those people (eg editors) who can help you establish a foot holding in the media arena.

5. Develop and utilise a media marketing plan. Identify your natural markets; your ideal clients and promote yourself actively within identified centres of influence.

CHAPTER NINE – THERE'S NO GAIN WITHOUT PAIN

If you are already achieving everything you set out to achieve in life and business then congratulations. But I rather suspect the reason you have invested in this book is because there are still things that are missing. If that is the case then I have a very poignant question for you.

How long do you want to live like this?

Thinking about this for a moment might mean thinking about ways you can change, for the better – even if it means making some sacrifices or having to suffer the possibility of rejection from time to time.

For most of us, the events in New York and Washington on 11th September 2001 will live with us, vividly, for the rest of our lives. But despite the terrible loss of life and the continuing problems those tragic events still cause, for many people, we always seem to find a way of bouncing back. Human beings are surprisingly resilient; particularly in the face of adversity.

I am sure we can all think of many events throughout the course of history that could have changed our lives or that did, in fact, shape a destiny. When I hear people complaining about the inadequacies of life and all the things that are seemingly working against them I ask that they put their problems into context. Those that have achieved any level of success have done so because of a fierce determination to succeed in spite of the occasional difficulty. One of the most uplifting experiences of my life was meeting Mark Peck, a much respected international speaker and trusted financial professional whose parents were told, when he was just three months old, that he was 'not expected to live long' and 'that for the period of time he did live he would be a helpless cripple'. Now married and with a family Mark still remains philosophical about his severe disabilities. He recounts, in a fabulous speech he made at both the Million Dollar Round Table meeting and Life Insurance Association (UK) Convention, that without those experiences he wouldn't be Mark Peck.

I am sure we all know someone who has suffered through severe ill health, bankruptcy or the death of a loved one but we really do have an in-built mechanism that helps us cope, adapt and even succeed in spite of those challenges. Sometimes we just don't know we have that strength and resilience.

Being strong – and maintaining that strength – is tough. Being a good leader, a business owner, a parent or someone that simply remains committed to the achievement of their goals is also tough. But no-one said it was easy. The individual who I can now call my very best client did not ask me to work with him until several months after I had been thrown out of his office for the third time! I didn't see the rejection: just that I recognised there was a business opportunity and he didn't (hence the reason for being thrown out of his office on three separate occasions) but I knew that if I was prepared to fight the battle in order to win the war I would eventually gain his trust.

Sometimes things don't get handed to us on a plate; we have to put up a fight. The individual who sees the bigger picture; who knows when to change direction (or get out of an office before they are thrown out!); who identifies problems and is ready to discuss solutions; who is accountable and who is confident in approach and attitude will make the most progress, because they are in control and accept they must adopt, adapt and accept change in order to stay ahead of the game. These people keep learning and picking up ideas wherever they can. Most importantly, they never ask people to do the things they wouldn't do.

So what is it about change that seems to cause so many people so many problems? Why it is so difficult to accept that something different today is such a radical step away from the known events of yesterday?

As we have already discussed, the challenges in life are just nature's way of testing our level of commitment. But if we think of change or a problem as a stumbling block, rather than a stepping stone, we are in trouble from the start.

Funnily enough, our children tend not to struggle with the same things we do. Why? Because, for the reasons outlined earlier, they have not yet formed opinions or reached conclusions about what we perceive to be positive or negative factors, because they are based on experience. Having spent three years as a manager within a large organisation I am now firmly of the opinion that problems are just a hook that many people choose to hang their coat on; mainly because they are a good – and generally accepted – excuse for failure. Some people focus on problems and complain about them for the simple reason that it's much easier to moan than eliminate the problem and move forward.

The biggest issue most of us face is change. As human beings, we are driven to seek control over our environment. We like to be able to predict, with some certainty, what will happen when we take action – and therefore be empowered to act. When we are in control we feel confident – and confidence is incredibly important. Therefore we are comfortable with all the things we know how to do; including, possibly, the ability to make a 'phone call to a prospect; to open or close a sale; to deal with a difficult client or to persist in the face of rejection and ask for a personal recommendation.

Whatever changes we have to face there will always be core elements of the new regime or environment we can feel confident in addressing. So, again, focus on the positive elements. In other words, think about what you can achieve and attempt to eliminate, possibly by delegating, the weaknesses. In the same way a skilled mountaineer would not attempt to scale a mountain in one climb – but would rather set a strategy in order to form a base camp and then climb, in stages, from that point – so it is with us. Identifying what we can deal with and then taking positive action will overcome even the things we previously saw as impossible tasks.

Motivation and persistence are great attributes to have when dealing with change. In the same way that athletes map out their annual calendar, selecting the events they need to enter then planning and managing their performance and activities according to their goals, so we should be looking to do the same. Good planning establishes very clear goals and enables us to remain focused. This, in turn, maximises our chances of success. It is also worth noting that changes within our own environment can also affect those of either our family or clients. So if others are used to us working in a certain way then we need to be especially careful in how we manage change, so that it has minimal impact on those people.

One other point worth noting is that so many people attempt to approach to a particular task on their own yet forget the basic principle: that it is much easier to work in a team. The old saying 'sticks in a bundle cannot be broken, those on their own can be broken by a child' applies, especially, in this example. But for some reason we are either reluctant to delegate or else feel that no-one can quite do the job as well as we can. Without making a commitment to empowering those around you and to maintaining training and therefore knowledge levels, which match our own, we will simply end up taking on more and more work – and the wheels and cogs of the business machine we have built will slowly grind to a halt over a period of time.

The perceived pain associated with running a business is not necessarily just about managing change. Having to pick up the telephone to make contact with a client whilst knowing there is every likelihood that we may get rejected is a skill that very few people naturally possess. Think again about the telephone call and awarding yourself marks out of ten, for each of the key component parts of that telephone call. What do we achieve by breaking things down into small, easily achievable, tasks? Well, I would suggest we have guaranteed ourselves nine points out of ten for every person we speak to on the telephone. Nine out of ten sounds like we have achieved something very close to perfection – and so we have. Why is it that the success or failure of a task has to be determined by the end point? So lets, perhaps, consider setting some goals based on the time we spend on a job rather than the results of the job.

THE SEVEN DEADLY SINS

Having looked at a number of key strategies and ideas to help in the development of a successful business practice let's look, for a moment, at the things we should definitely be trying to avoid if we are to reach those goals.

FIRST - No Order and organisation. I have often heard the phrase 'tidy life, tidy mind' and I am sure it is true. Sometimes people love disorder but is it because they can then hide in it? An untidy desk, cluttered diary, disheveled appearance or disregard for the importance of punctuality betrays the individual who is not in control of their business. Most of us hate paperwork but we must embrace the administrative process and adopt high standards as a route to an achievable, sustainable, goal.

SECOND – No business strategy. Ask yourself whether your business runs you or whether you run it? Do you know when you are going to exit the business (maybe through retirement or trade sale) or do you find yourself just running ever faster to keep up with the changing demands of the profession? Plan a route out – even if you decide to stay on when you get to that pre-determined point. Without a strategy your business will only ever be worth what it is today.

THIRD – No hotel days. If you are serious about implementing either the ideas in this book or your own then you need time for reflection and to plan. Allocate some of the time you have put aside to those people you work with and you can, and will, pick up a lot of very good feedback from group discussions.

FOURTH – No primary purpose. Every successful individual in the world will tell you this is one of the key ingredients to a successful outcome. Vision and focus are amongst the most important of all disciplines.

FIFTH – No balance. In the next chapter we will look at the importance of having a rounded, well-managed life; including taking time out for maintaining good personal health, spending time with the family and for pursing other hobbies and interests. However tempting, do not be a 'slave' to your business.

SIXTH – No black and white integrity. This is not just about the way we conduct ourselves as professionals but the way we are with ourselves. How often are we brutally honest about how we are doing in life? How often do we break promises to ourselves, those we love and to our clients?

SEVENTH – Not going through the front door. The front door in life involves commitment and a determination to meet problems head on. Using the back door is the easy way in because we can often pass through it unnoticed. To truly succeed we sometimes need to understand there is no gain without pain.

Dealing with the problems and issues that every-day life throws at us has never been easy; nor will it get any easier. But as human beings we have an in-built mechanism which is designed to self-preserve. Think about the stories we have all read in the newspapers about the mother, 120lb in weight, who single-handedly lifted a motor car to free her trapped child underneath? Consider those that suffer terrible illness or appalling injuries and have to immediately and radically adapt to their new circumstances in order to survive. If we did not possess this ability to fight in the face of difficulty these things would simply not happen.

These stories, or a personal experience like them, put the challenges we all face, every day, into some sort of perspective. Is contacting our top 20 clients and asking them for help in developing our business contacts so difficult? What stops us making the telephone call that might be the start of a great new relationship with a client? What stops us filling our diary with new meetings; to communicating better; to contributing to a team environment in our home or office and what stops us fulfilling those dreams and ambitions? Whilst I think we are all still searching for the answer one thing is for sure. Only we can determine the future and only we can make a difference.

If you risk nothing you risk everything…………

Quotes

'Work smarter. If you make a sale don't take time off to celebrate. Instead, look at it as motivation to sell more whilst you are on a roll. Make appointments when your mood is positive. The more people you see the better. Which is better, a hundred percent of twenty deals or twenty percent of a hundred deals.

"There's always an Apocalypse Du Jour."

"Whoever said it's not whether you win or lost that counts; probably lost!"

"Life involves constant change – you must change and grow daily, weekly, yearly. If you refuse to grow, you will die. If not physically then emotionally."

"Winning isn't everything – but wanting to win is."

"You must recognise your obligations to yourself, to your family, your customer, your company and, most of all, to your prospect."

"You owe it to your prospect to improve his or her life or business if your product or service can provide the means. You also owe it to yourself, for the sake of your own self-image."

TAKING ACTION

1. Using the Masterplan, overleaf, decide upon all your personal and professional objectives. Write down what you want from this month; what time off you will have, what issues are causing problems and what standards need to be improved. Use the Masterplan to commit to, and stay in touch with, all the goals you have set whilst reading this book.

2. Using the Business Analysis (following the Masterplan) award a score for each of the business disciplines (change them to suit) and commit to do the same every three months. This will help you to focus on the progress you are making. If you are, reward yourself.

   *Any score that falls into the Black Zone needs to be addressed immediately; the Light Grey Zone indicates an acceptable level of performance (but requires continual monitoring) and the Mid-Grey Zone indicates peak performance.

3. Set yourself a goal to make at least ten calls you've been meaning to make for a while. Mark yourself out of ten for each call (three for picking up the receiver; three for dialling the number; three for having a conversation and one for an appointment). Reward yourself for a score of ninety or better.

Month

THIS MONTH-MASTERPLAN

Primary Objective

Strategic Objective

Personal Development

Personality

Prospecting

Irritating Items (use pencil)

1.
2.
3.
4.
5.
6.
7.
8.
9.
10.

Week	Target	Ach'd

Time Off

Improving Standards This Month

Home

Traits

Self confidence	happiness
personal effectiveness	progress
order and org	backlog
time control	mindchan
new doors	prospect
keeping agree	biz=fun

MindChangers

Hotel days this year

Exercicse

Do & HaveThis Month

Eight Objectives	Done
1.	
2.	
3.	
4.	
5.	
6.	
7.	
8.	

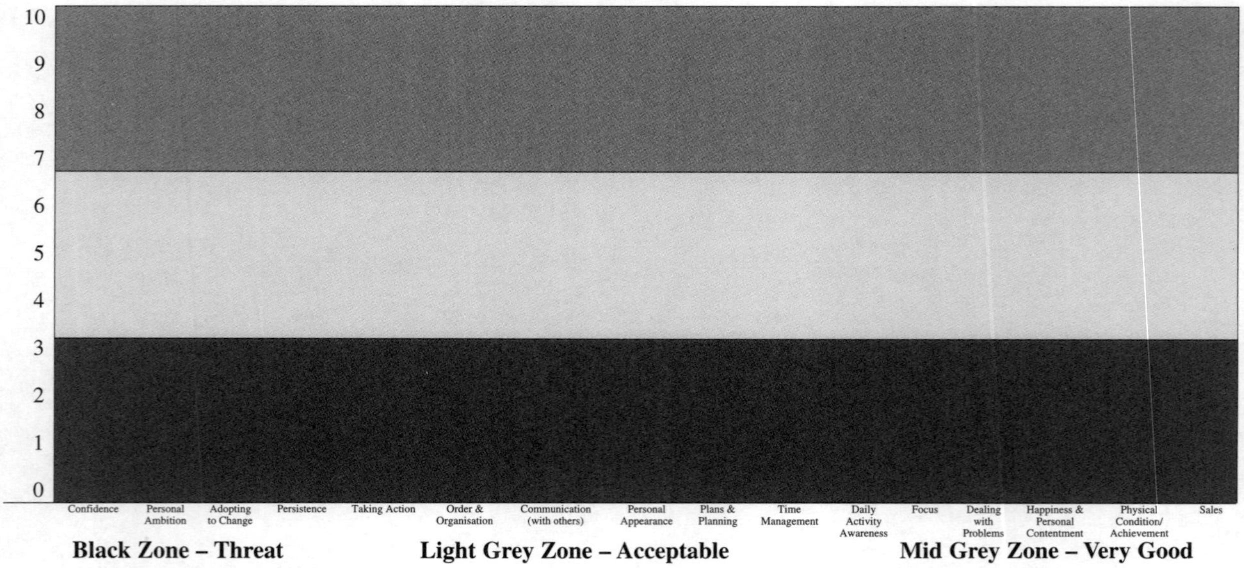
10
9
8
7
6
5
4
3
2
1
0
Confidence
Personal Ambition
Adopting to Change
Persistence
Taking Action
Order & Organisation
Communication (with others)
Personal Appearance
Plans & Planning
Time Management
Daily Activity Awareness
Focus
Dealing with Problems
Happiness & Personal Contentment
Physical Condition/ Achievement
Sales
Black Zone – Threat
Light Grey Zone – Acceptable
Mid Grey Zone – Very Good

120

CHAPTER TEN-THE ULTIMATE BALANCING ACT

We all seem to spend so much time on the "business" competencies of our profession that we often neglect the "human" matters – our relationships and, especially, our families. That support system is the foundation on which we build our careers so it is critical for us to constantly be aware of our priorities; always making enough time for these relationships. Otherwise, our careers may crumble along with our self-esteem.

Sadly "family relationships" are not usually considered to be important within the daily grind and chaos we call business, Yet, this focus exemplifies the very essence of what we speak about (the important things in life) and the quality of our family relationships directly impacts the bottom lines of our businesses. Just as secure, happy, employees make a more productive workplace so do happy, cared-for, supported advisers make more productive salespeople.

The Box

If you begin some family traditions that revolve around travel, you will find that they take some of the pain of separation away.

When I began travelling because of my business, I decided to give each of my children a box. Instead of bringing them a big, expensive, present every time I travelled I carried on a family tradition that a friend had started on her travels. That is, I bring each of my children some small item that is a symbol of the city or country I visited, which they'd put in their boxes. Some of the things I have brought them include a miniature pair of clogs from Amsterdam and a small metal gondola from Venice.

These gifts are fun to find, inexpensive, and easy to tuck into the corner of a suitcase. Not only do the children have something to look forward to when I return from a trip, but they also learn something special about each of my destinations.

Things To Tell Dad Notebook

Another thing I did to stay close with my children when I had to travel was to give them a "Things to Tell Dad" notebook. I picked a special notebook for each of them with something on the cover that they loved, and I told them to keep that notebook with them every day and write down anything they wanted to tell me about. Every night when I called home, they would have their notebook lists as a reminder of what had happened during the day. I think they told me more because of those notebooks than they would have if I had been at home!

Chart the Course

We have a large, wall-mounted, map of the world so that each time I travel, the children put a coloured pin in the place I will be. It is a fun way to connect them to my trip and also to see how many places I have been.

Travel Tips

Here are some travel tips to help minimise the stress of business travel on both traveller and family.

- Carefully analyse the purpose of each trip; say "no" to unnecessary ones.
- Draw travel "boundaries" as a family, deciding how much travel is excessive.
- Maintain reasonable intervals between trips, if possible.
- Don't travel on weekends.
- Don't travel on special occasions, such as birthdays and anniversaries.
- Telephone home each day.

- Take one hour off each day when you are on the road to be alone, relax, exercise or do something new and different.

- Schedule weekly relationship time on your calendar.

- Take loved ones on business trips occasionally.

- When you come home, listen before you share the details of your journey.

Children love receiving letters. If you have to be away from home, drop them a line. Telling your children that you love them and showing physical affection as often as possible is also a basic human need and moulds, to a considerable extent, the character of that child.

The big question is whether we work long hours irrespective of need. How often do we find ourselves passing up the opportunity to read a story or spend time with other members of our family because we simply thought we had to 'finish a job off?' Whilst business matters may be a tremendous burden from time to time there is always a time in the day or week to develop family traditions; possibly an evening where the whole family sits around the dinner table. Or a Sunday afternoon stroll? Or a 'picnic' night when the children get to choose what they want to eat? Rob Parsons, one of the best speakers I have ever heard on the subject of balancing business and family time, has been a tremendous source of inspiration; to the point where I now see the real value in spending as much time as possible with those that are dear to me. Remember, if your child is ten years old, 3,650 days have already gone so you have only 2,920 left. Sobering thought isn't it? Think of all the urgent calls you have ever received or the tasks you were asked to do: were any of them so urgent they couldn't wait at least five minutes? Don't allow yourself to say things like 'There will soon be a time when I can slow down' or 'I'm working as hard as I am for the kids'. As Rob Parsons says 'By trying to give our kids what we didn't have, we forgot to give them what we did have'.

I have experienced a quite an amazing transformation in the behaviour and general relationship I have with my children simply because I tell them things like I believe in them and that I constantly try to catch them doing something right, rather than wrong. The same is true in business. Colleagues, clients and other business associates will always react far more positively and be more committed to helping us grow and develop if we adopt these same basic principles in the relationship. Ask yourself what you would want to do differently if you were married to yourself. Perhaps, even, what you would do if you knew this was your last day on earth. Many of us will never be fortunate enough to live a long and fulfilling life so why take the chance of not living each day in the best possible way?

If we had a sense of urgency, remained focused and could achieve something approaching a sensible balance in life, how good would we feel? So I have to ask the question, why isn't this happening already or why can't it happen at this point? To start with, consider the following process and if you can't think of any good reasons not to implement and action them today then please at least give them a try:

1. What have I accomplished so far? Reviewing and acknowledging your past successes are very important to maintain confidence levels and to fuel desire and determination.

2. What has been my biggest disappointment? Putting these into perspective, especially with regard to successes achieved, can often lead to the conclusion that things aren't quite as bad as was first envisaged.

3. What have I learned? We all make mistakes and have disappointments but these are all good experiences if the lessons to be learned from them are turned into plans to prevent the same mistake happening again.

4. How do I limit myself and how can I stop? As individuals we are the only ones to restrict our success.

5. What are my personal values? Most of us feel better if we are doing things we perceive to be good.

6. What is my role in life? Failed success can provide the ability to have the things you want but balance is equally important. You cannot put your life 'on hold' whilst you decide.

7. What will I focus on next? Knowing that you have the ideas and strategies to always get what you focus on helps build a determined way of generating results.

8. What are my goals? There is nothing wrong with setting the highest goals; especially when you can justify it by reaching the target. The main attention of your focus (the goals) may be something quite challenging but break it down into small manageable pieces and start from there.

9. What are my top six goals? Use the 6:4:1 method, described earlier in this book, to help make achievement and results attainable.

10. How can I achieve those results? Part of the plan is confidence and this only comes from practice. Keep persevering with all the best ideas you currently have and then add some more (maybe from this book?) in order to achieve a successful outcome. Too many of us spend all our time focusing on problems when, in fact, we should be spending no more than 10% of our time on the problems and 90% of our time on the solution.

There is no doubt that creating synergy in life, including work family and health, can have a positive influence on production. When we have balance in our lives everything we do, we do better. And if we think all of this is impossible then let's consider, from time to time, going back to basics. Sometimes there is more fulfillment to be had in life by stepping sideways, or even backwards, so long as we subscribe to the theory we should be setting personal goals before business goals. Success is more than making money. Successful people know this because they don't find time, they make time. Life is so much simpler when we know what is essential.

The Story of the Carpenter

Isn't it strange how we seem to set much higher standards for ourselves than for others? At this point, I am reminded of a story, about an elderly carpenter, which illustrates this point:

'An elderly carpenter was ready to retire. He told his employer of his plans to leave the house/building business and live a more leisurely life with his wife enjoying his extended family.

He would miss the pay-cheque, but he needed to retire. They could get by.

The contractor was sorry to see his good worker go and asked if he could build one more house as a personal favour. The carpenter said yes but in time it was easy to see that his heart was not in his work. He allowed his workmanship to become shoddy and he started to use inferior materials. It was an unfortunate way to end a dedicated career.

When the carpenter finished his work the employer came to inspect the house. He handed the front-door key to the carpenter and said 'My gift to you'. The carpenter was shocked,. What a shame! If only he had known he was building his own house, he would have done it all so differently.

So it is with us. We build our lives, a day at a time, often putting less than our best into the building. Then with a shock we realise we have to live in the house we have built. If we could do it all over again we would do it so differently. But we cannot go back.

You are the carpenter. Each day you hammer a nail, place a board or erect a wall. Life is a do-it-yourself project. Your attitudes and the choices you make today builds the house you live in tomorrow. So build wisely!

Quotes

"Commitment in every activity, especially professional selling, is one of the most important ingredients necessary if you are to succeed and be content in your success. We live by choice, not by chance."

"Attitude is a choice, the most important one you will ever make."

"Habits are the key to all success."

"Kind words cost little, but accomplish much."

"Real motivation comes from within."

"Goals are dreams with deadlines."

"No-one else can raise your self-esteem."

"No-one was ever heard to say on the death bed, 'I wish I had spent more time at the office'."

"If we listen to them when they are five, six or seven years old, they may listen to us when they are fifteen, sixteen or seventeen."

TAKING ACTION

1. Write down a master dream list. List all the things you want to do, be, have, or go to in your lifetime. Pick one dream to do each year with your family.

2. When appraising performance, whether that of a child or a business colleague, start by giving them the highest grade possible. Then ask them to write a letter, as if it was the end of the year, describing what they did to justify the grade.

3. Make sure you pass onto your children the most significant lesson you learned from your father, mother or older person you knew as a child.

4. Take time out to teach your children how to handle money. Help them prepare a simple income and expenditure budget and keep track of it.

5. Take your child or loved one to the place where you work. Let them sit or stand in your place and tell them how you spend your day.

6. Catch your children doing something right – today.

7. Watch one of their favourite television programmes and try to appreciate why they like it.

8. At the next possible opportunity, take a half day. Spend it with those who are important to you.

9. Promise that you will never give up on the relationship with your child or loved one – whatever age they are – even if they have left home under a cloud.

10. Make a list of values that are important to you. Ask yourself whether you are effectively passing those onto your child.

CHAPTER TWELVE – THE TWELVE KEY SUCCESS FACTORS

What follows is a summary of everything we have covered in this book. If it helps you to remember the points, copy it and put it somewhere prominent.

1. **Activity:** Motion in a set direction that builds and builds in the direction you seek.

2. **Regime:** A daily diet of good habits that brings stabilises your being.

3. **Escape to Freedom:** A detailed Masterplan of your route to the final winning post.

4. **Action now:** The immediate application of your gut felt vision to secure your future desires.

5. **Future now:** The act of playing out what you want now, guarantees its future arrival.

6. **Inner Image:** Polish up who you are and inspire yourself to new heights.

7. **Mindchangers:** Turn the keys in your mind and open the door to all possibility.

8. **Order:** Creates the positive foundation for change.

9. **New Horizons:** Doing what others refuse to do puts you at the top of the 'Success' waiting list.

10. **Practise:** Being an expert in your chosen arena automatically creates the opportunity of unlimited success.

11. **Fear:** Fear is life gauging your commitment.

12. **Now:** Enjoy the moment and never forget.

AND FINALLY........

I hope you have got – and will continue to get – considerable value and success from the ideas in this book.

But I have a word of warning: if you are not prepared to seriously work towards your life's dreams, add this book to your stack of texts that represent a feeble attempt at change. However, if you are fed up with frustration, anxieties, broken promises and going without much of what you think you deserve then commit, today, to change.

I don't have the answers to your life – you do. Somewhere inside you is the potential for greatness. The choice to be great, or to leave your unlimited potential behind you in a wooden box, is your decision.

Good luck!